Gadgets!

THE ULTIMATE
CATALOG FOR
GADGET LOVERS

Martin Schwartz

PHAROS
BOOKS

A SCRIPPS HOWARD COMPANY

NEW YORK, NEW YORK

A QUARTO BOOK

First published in 1986 by
Pharos Books
A Scripps Howard Company
200 Park Avenue
New York, New York 10166

Distributed in the United States by
Ballantine Books, a division of Random House, Inc.
and in Canada by Random House of Canada, Ltd.

Library of Congress Catalog Card Number: 85-052318
Pharos Books ISBN: 0-88687-271-5
Ballantine Books ISBN: 0-345-33721-2

GADGETS! The Ultimate Catalog for Gadget Lovers
was prepared and produced by
Quarto Marketing Ltd.
15 West 26th Street
New York, New York 10010

Editor: Felecia Abbadessa
Designer: Ron Gonzalez
Photo Researcher: Susan M. Duane

Typeset by BPE Graphics, Inc.
Color separations by Hong Kong Scanner Craft Company Ltd.
Printed and bound in Hong Kong by Leefung-Asco Printers Ltd.

ABOUT THE AUTHOR

A confirmed gadget addict, author Martin Schwartz was an investigator with the New York City Department of Consumer Affairs. He later became an urban affairs, investigative television reporter with WKBW-TV, the ABC affiliate in Buffalo, New York. Martin Schwartz was recently a contributing editor and columnist for a number of media trade publications. He now supports his gadget habit by freelance writing, editing and by producing industrial videos for Fortune 500 corporations.

CONTENTS

INTRODUCTION

By the time you finish reading the introduction, at least one of the gadgets described in this book should be out of date. Every minute, someone around the world stumbles across a solution to one of life's many challenges. Whether it's building a better mousetrap, or creating a new leisure-time comfort, man's quest for quality and inventive craftsmanship runs deep.

This book attempts to locate those special gadgets and labor saving devices that stand out in today's marketplace: gadgets that are unique in their approach to manual and mechanical work or leisure and playtime activities. Some items may be so simple that you'll scratch your head in disbelief. Others employ state-of-the-art technologies developed in the world's most sophisticated laboratories. A few are just outrageous.

Many of the gadgets' futuristic features were originally created for space and military applications. Only now are they emerging in the consumer market. But the impact of these computerized microprocessors and digital products is revolutionizing our lifestyles. Computers are automatizing not only office and industrial work but also simple household functions such as turning on and shutting off lights. Cleaning jobs that once required chemicals or poisons now use sound and magnetic energy. The Brave New World has come of age.

Therefore, to place the selected items within some context, this book is structured by chapters using the rooms in your house as a guide. Quite honestly, there is no set selection pattern for chosing products. I chose only what caught my eye. But since many gadgets have multiple uses, you should check every possible chapter

if you're looking for a particular piece.

Most of these products are not available in stores, even the largest outlets. They are, however, available through mail-order catalogs. There are virtually hundreds of them for every conceivable purpose and pleasure. I have provided a listing of the most popular catalogs in the appendix so that you too can have access to their offerings.

Manufacturers and inventors contact these catalog companies and attempt to sell them on their gadgets, either through trade shows or direct approach. They want the item included in the listings. Although some manufacturers do market to the public directly, for most, if they're not carried by the major catalogs, chances are that a product won't make it. Competition is fierce and many of the big outfits, such as Hammacher Schlemmer, Innovations, and The Sharper Image, do extensive testing to substantiate a company's claims or to select the best of

competing models. It's no surprise that some of the best gadgets are carried by five or six catalogs.

To describe the various products mentioned in the book, I relied on information supplied either by the manufacturer or the mail order catalog, known throughout the book as the "distributor." Neither the publisher nor I am qualified to render a technical evaluation on each gadget, since it would be virtually impossible to check out each item. Therefore, we have taken the sellers' descriptions of their products at face value. But don't you, unless you know the product or manufacturer intimately. If you are considering buying something listed here, ask questions when you order. Remember, in the time it takes to write and publish this book, some items may have added new features or begun using a technology you don't like. Don't be afraid to probe for specifics. You'll be amazed with what you can learn in the process and by what you'll end up with.

The Kitchen Gadgets

PULL TOP OPENER

If you're worried about breaking nails, or are just a nut about exerting yourself, consider the Pull Top can opener. Just place the plastic holder around the can's tab and lift. If you're injured or have arthritis and don't have fine muscle control in your fingers, this device is a big help. **(E)**

SELF CHILLING BUTTER DISH

Picky about your bread and butter? We all enjoy starting a meal just right. Well, this Swiss device keeps butter cool, firm, and fresh for up to three hours on the table. A special freezing mechanism within the unit's hardwood base cools two sticks or one large block of butter. It makes good sense for parties or for those perfectionists who demand that every part of the meal be served flawlessly. **(I)**

CORDLESS FOOD WARMER

Keep those dishes piping hot right at your table without tripping over the electric cord. Your guests will be quite impressed when they go for seconds from this West German server. Inside the unit, a block of quartz sand is heated to 248 F (120 C) by an electric coil that gets plugged into any wall outlet. Just remove the plug, and the nickel plated steel exterior stays hot for up to half an hour after serving. The 14½" x 17½" (36.8 cm x 44.4 cm) area holds one large or two medium sized dishes. **(I)**

ELECTRIC ICE CREAM SCOOP

Your mouth salivates as that luscious ice cream comes out of the fridge. With anxious glee, you dig your spoon into what you imagine to be a delightfully creamy texture. But suddenly, that heightened smile of anticipation turns into a horrified frown as the spoon bends in half, extracting only a flaky, miniscule portion. Yes, you've been foiled by ice cream overhardness. What can put your faith back into that lost childhood experience of licking fresh ice cream? Try the Electric Ice Cream Scoop, designed for both home and commercial use. This modern electric device lets you serve perfectly formed scoops of hard ice cream without waiting for it to thaw. A 248 F (120 C) preheated, non-stick, Teflon coated, aluminum bowl makes the toughest containers of ice cream melt into a special scoop of your favorite flavor. The device plugs into any outlet. Don't struggle with rock-hard ice cream any longer. Get those delicious childhood licks while you still can. **(I)**

ELECTRIC SELF-STIRRING SAUCE PAN

A gourmet's delight. Difficult-to-make sauces become easy. The built-in blade rotates at 85 RPM to keep just the right consistency. The variable five position thermostat can be set from 95 F (35 C) to 311 F (155 C) and for everything from hollandaise to béarnaise. Comes with a recipe book. **(I)**

FLEXPORT, VARIOUS MODEL SIZES

You've had a beautiful evening and are lying in bed the next morning recalling some of the highlights. Suddenly, right in the middle of that early morning reverie, "Fido" wants to go outside. Not content to wait, he scratches, he barks, he jumps up and down on your bedroom door—just about everything possible to ruin the mood. If you live in a private house, why be a slave to your pets' bathroom needs? This Flexport unit allows your pets outside access when they want it.

You can also stop worrying about getting "Tabby" in from the rain. The plastic triangular fans push to the side so your pets can come and go as they please. There'll be no more accidents on that rug just because you stayed out late. The device closes up to a tight fit so that drafts, bugs, and other undesirables can't get inside. It's maintenance free and completely weatherproof. Sleep much more satisfied, knowing your pets can get relief—by themselves. **(M)**

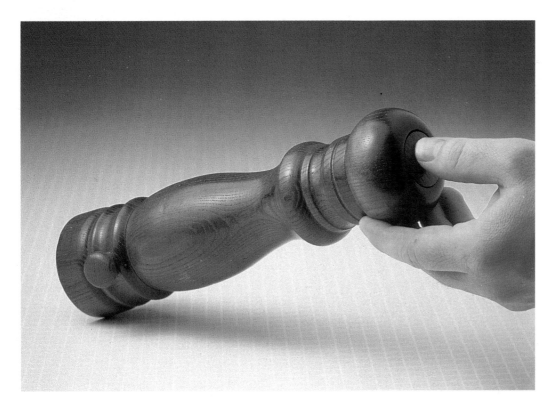

CORDLESS ELECTRIC PEPPER MILL

Give your dinner guests the ultimate in a salad or pasta experience. If you think a restaurant has class when the waiter circles the table offering freshly ground pepper, then this device will make you a real bon vivant. A battery operated grinding mechanism rotates at 65 RPM to make freshly ground pepper at the touch of a button. Don't look foolish standing there grinding and twisting. This quiet device holds up to 20 grams of peppercorns. It's easily refilled by unscrewing the wooden plug. The Pepper Mill is made of a carved and polished Japanese Keyaki hardwood, and comes with batteries. **(I)**

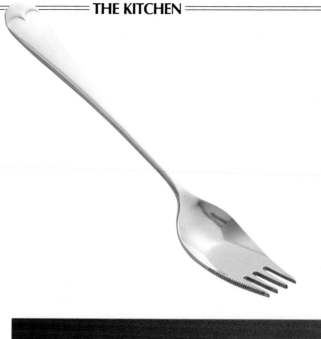

THREE-IN-ONE BUFFET UTENSIL

It's a knife, a fork, and a spoon all rolled into one. The curved bowl fork also functions as a spoon. A serrated edge works like a knife. **(I)**

LA VALTROMPLINA NUT AND BEAN ROASTER

You know the great taste of roasted chestnuts in winter. But if you buy them on city streets, more often than not you get burned or inferior nuts. Like to roast them at home? Remember when you forgot to check the oven? Nobody likes their nuts completely black. Now you can get that warm wintery feeling without worry and waste. This unique roaster can prepare chestnuts, peanuts, pumpkin and sunflower seeds, cashews, pecans, and countless other high protein snacks without adding unwanted flavors or calories. It can also roast coffee beans because it uses no cooking oil. A motor-driven, 8" (20.3 cm) diameter steel ball automatically rotates within the aluminum frame to roast the contents on all sides. The unit controls the temperature, so there's no chance of burning. **(M)**

TOASTESS ELECTRIC KETTLE

Tea time. If you work in an office and are tired of running out for that cup of tea or coffee, then this kettle will keep you at your desk. It doesn't need a stove. Plug the Toastess Electric Kettle into any 110-volt AC outlet and it boils more than four cups of hot water in a moment. You don't even have to think about the device if you want to keep water boiling since the thermostatically-controlled kettle shuts off automatically when it boils dry. Just add more water at your own convenience and it resets. Don't forget the crumpets. **(I)**

CAPE COD OYSTER AND CLAM OPENERS

You're in the fish store staring at those fresh clams. The price is right, but you're afraid to struggle with sharp knives to force them open. No longer. These oyster and clam tools let you pry open shells safely and quickly. A special oyster blade contains a sharp ¾" (1.9 cm) point to force the "pearls" open. The sharp clam blade cuts right through that tough muscle. Made of stainless steel, they both come with a 5" x 7" (12.7 x 17.8 cm) maple base. **(I)**

ELECTRIC PASTA MAKER

Mama never had it so good. Make up to 1½ lbs (.681 kg) of fresh pasta in just ten minutes. This kitchen device mixes and extrudes pasta dough in a single chamber so you don't need to transfer dough from bowl to bowl. A built-in blower helps dry the pasta so pieces won't stick. It's equipped with eleven pasta dies; enabling you to make spaghetti, vermicelli, fettucine, linguine, lasagna, ziti, small macaroni, and gnocchi. There are even dies for cookies, bagels, pretzels, and breadsticks. The 155-watt, ¼ HP, fan-cooled motor turns the mixing arm to blend ingredients quickly. A safety switch shuts the motor off when you lift the lid. Easy cleaning with soap and water. There's a measuring cup, and an instruction book containing fourteen recipes. Buon Appetito!... **(I)**

CABINET JAR OPENER

The ultimate kitchen time-saver. We've all struggled with jammed up jars and screw-off containers. But remember that broken glass and sprained wrist? The design of this jar opener lets you remove almost any jar top without any trouble. It can adjust to twist-off tops from ⅜" (2.5 cm) diameter to 5" (12.7 cm). The harder you turn, the tighter it grips. It mounts beneath a cabinet, out of sight but conveniently ready for use. (C)

MICROWAVE TESTER

Worried about cancer in the kitchen? Many people still resist buying timesaving microwave ovens for just that reason. With this ingenious device, you can warm up those leftovers without fear. Just pass this molded acrylic sensor around the door and hinge of your microwave. If there's a leak, a brilliant red light lets you know. If you place the device in various spots inside, you'll know whether the wave pattern is cooking evenly. **(C)**

WORLD'S ONLY CORDLESS ELECTRIC CARVING KNIFE

Reportedly, this is the only electric carving knife that operates without a cord. You can cut up that roast quickly, right at your table. Whether indoors or on the porch, there's no need to slice meat or chicken all at once. Why let food flavors and juices escape, turning the meat cold? The carver's 8" (20.3 cm), serrated, stainless steel blades operate at two thousand strokes per minute to glide through your meat quickly. A 4.8-volt DC motor operates up to thirty minutes on a full twenty-four hour charge. Just recharge the removable battery pack as needed. With this device there's no need to run to the kitchen for seconds. **(I)**

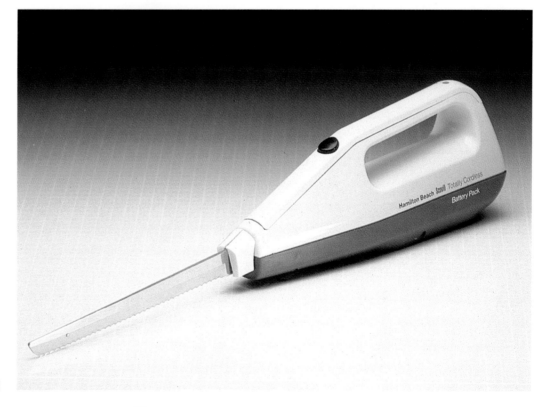

PROFESSIONAL CHEF'S THERMOMETER

Most food thermometers cook right along with the item. Unfortunately, some may conduct unwanted heat, or make a hole for juices to escape, especially with meat. Try this professional device. Take that steak out of the oven and immediately probe the inside. With dough or sauces, you'll get precise readings to get your food just right. **(I)**

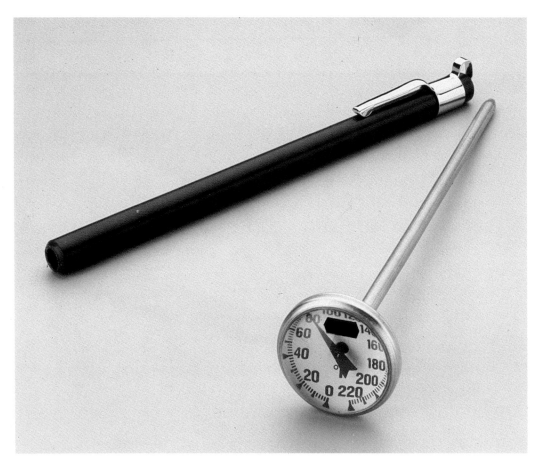

MUG MATE

Tired of drinking cold coffee just because you can't gulp it down quickly? Whether you're relaxing over the morning paper, or trying to complete some office work, a hot cup of tea or coffee hits the spot. Don't waste the contents or spend money just to get a fresh cup. Mug Mate will keep your coffee hot to the last drop. Just plug it in, place the mug on its base, and you can safely relax with piping hot beverages. Don't worry, it won't bring the liquid to a boil. **(C)**

PORTABLE MINI-STOVE

A must if you live in a dorm or are renting an efficiency type hotel room when traveling. This appliance performs all the cooking functions of a full-sized range in as little space as an ordinary hot plate. It broils, boils, toasts, warms, grills, and defrosts; in fact, it can perform up to three separate functions simultaneously. The 5" (12.7 cm) diameter, 700-watt stovetop burner has an adjustable dial so you can heat soup, make coffee, fry eggs, and even sauté that favorite French sauce. In the lower compartment, the adjustable 800-watt oven broils meats and grills open-faced sandwiches on the two-piece broiling pan. There's also an open upper grill for toasting or warming. This can be replaced by a tray to create another burner. The oven temperature can then rise to 600 F (315.5 C) for quick cooking. With sturdy chrome and steel, this Portable Mini-Stove is a must for that weekend house in the woods. (I)

GARLIC JAR

Garlic, one of the most important flavorings in good cooking, often becomes stale and soft from improper storage. This charming, practical garlic house is a must for cooks and garlic lovers who crave the pungent taste that only the freshest garlic can give. Hand-painted with delicate, colorful flowers, this earthenware jar keeps garlic fresher, longer. Its dark interior keeps the garlic from sprouting while the air holes provide enough ventilation to keep it dry. Made in Italy, this product makes a useful and decorative addition to any kitchen. It's also terrific for storing shallots and ginger. 6" (15.24 cm) high. Keep the snap and the freshness in your seasonings. **(C)**

TOMATO PRESS

Nothing tastes better than homemade tomato sauce but many cooks are put off by the process of pureeing tomatoes and settle for canned or bottled sauces. This professional, quality tomato press takes the mess and hassle out of doing it yourself. Just pop in whole tomatoes, turn the handle and the puree pours out from one chute, the skins and seeds from another. Great for making soups, too, this fire-engine red press will help you prepare tantalizing sauces just like Mom's. You'll never use canned sauces again. **(I)**

OIL AND VINEGAR SERVER

For salad lovers who like their salads just right, this Italian designed oil and vinegar server pours a perfectly blended dressing. The dial can be set to suit any taste. Pour only oil or vinegar, or any of three proportions in between. This two-section pitcher holds generous portions of oil and vinegar and is great for storing between meals. Attractively designed, each compartment is made of clear, sturdy acrylic and the lid and separate spill-proof tray are tough, red ABS plastic. At 7" (17.78 cm) high, this server fits right in with any table setting. **(C)**

The Pantry

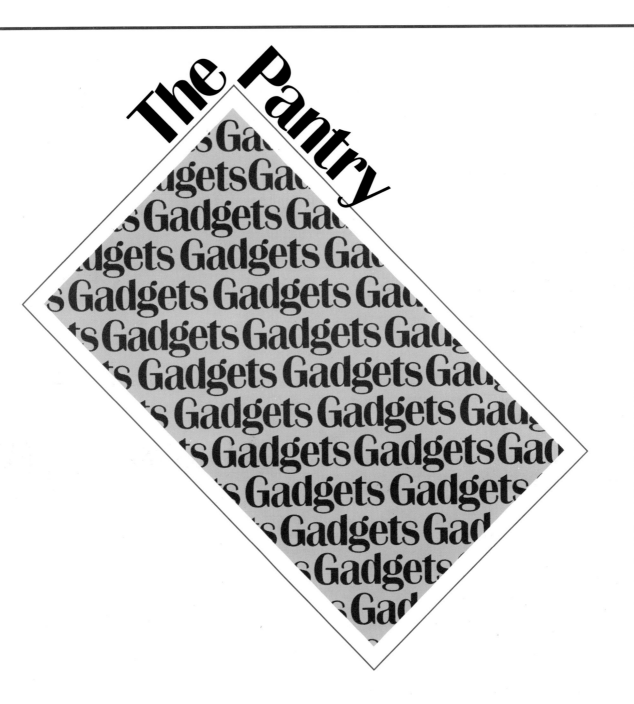

Gadgets Gadgets Gadgets Gadgets Gadgets Gadgets Gadgets Gadgets Gadgets Gadgets Gadgets Gadgets

COMPUCAL NUTRITION COMPUTER

It's a computerized kitchen scale that weighs food in pounds and metric units, up to 5 lbs (2.27 kg). With diet being so important today in avoiding chemical-based cancers and other industrial killers, this device can give you a digital readout of all the calories, sodium, carbohydrates, protein, cholesterol, and fat for any sized food portion. The memory allows up to nine family members to keep a cumulative total of their food intake simply by punching in a pre-programmed code. It also allows you to check the nutritional content of a recipe before preparation. Information is stored on more than six-hundred of the most popular generic and name brand food items. An automatic shut-off feature activates twenty seconds after your last entry. You are what you eat! **(M)**

KOOL MATE

Going to the beach, or taking a ski outing into the mountains? It's great to have that cool beverage or that cup of hot soup available when you want it. Whether hot or cold, this special device will keep your food and beverages at just the right temperature. For cooling, just plug the unit into any cigarette lighter... while you drive that case of Budweiser gets perfectly chilled. For that cup of hot soup on the slopes, two small thermo-electric modules replace the refrigerator coils and compressor. It's made of insulated, high-impact plastic with a seamless aluminum liner. A 12-volt motor is permanently lubricated, according to the distributor, for trouble-free usage. **(I)**

BOODABOX ODOR FREE LITTER BOX

Does your kitchen ever smell like a leaky cesspool? Sometimes the cat's litter box emits a particularly obnoxious odor that will drive more than mice out of the house. On occasion, the cats will also unknowingly spread litter remains around while trying to cover them up. With this Odor-Free Litter Box, you'll forget about these unpleasant problems. The unit's 72 sq in. (464.54 sq cm) high vent contains a charcoal air filter. Fresh air flows in and only fresh air flows out. The replaceable filter lasts three to six months. This self-enclosed container also ends scatter problems. Your cat enters through a leak proof sealed canopy. Keep a lid on that odor. **(I)**

GAGGIA ELECTRIC DISTILLER

They say that the alchemists no longer practice their art, but if that old gypsy living alone up in the hills had had this device two hundred years ago, modern science may have sung a different song. With the Gaggia Distiller, you can extract flavors, oils, and scents from flowers, fruits, herbs, or any other organic material.

Make your own concoctions, beauty aids, perfumes, and other potions that you practice with in your homemade crafts. The electrical mechanism heats as much as 1¼ l of any liquid of organic material at gradually rising temperatures. The device slowly extracts the desired flavor or scent as vapor. Then the vapor passes through a Pyrex condenser, cooled by three liters of continuously circulated water. The distillate is collected in a separate flask. Its purity is assured by the use of copper and glass tubing and brass fittings. There's an 18-watt fan to cool circulating water. A built-in thermometer helps you determine optimum temperatures at which various flavors vaporize. **(E)**

The Dining Room

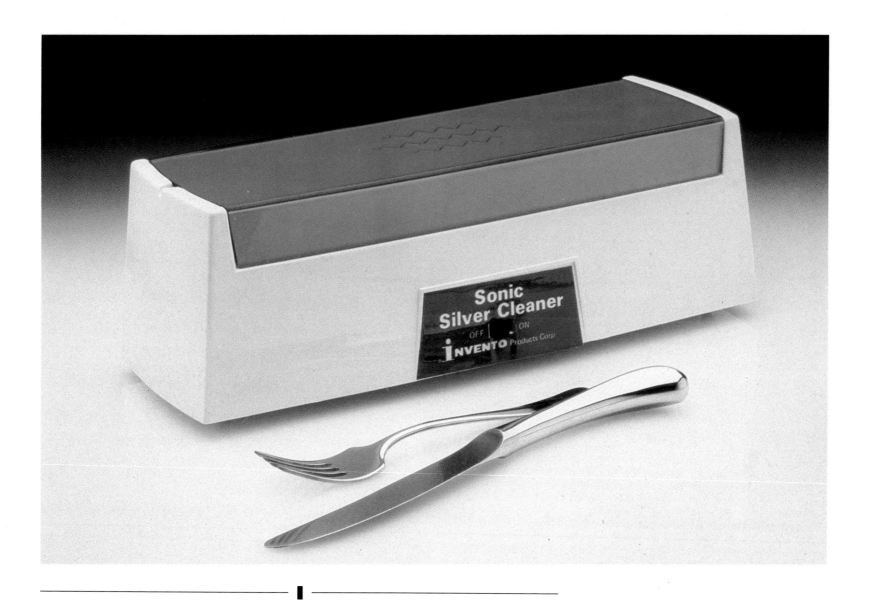

SONIC SILVER CLEANER

Sick of seeing your fine silver or silver-plated utensils tarnish before your eyes? Why waste hours polishing? This device will clean up your silverware in seconds, without elbow grease or abrasives that can wear away at metal. It uses low frequency sound waves of sixty cycles per second to create electrolytic action. This helps the special cleaning solution remove tarnish. This gadget is perfectly safe for antique finishes, and cleans an entire six-piece setting at once. It comes with a 12 oz (354.88 ml) bottle of reusable liquid cleaner. Get that silver shine that only sound can give. **(I)**

ELECTRIC PLATE BLANKET

Getting food served on a warm plate adds something special to a meal. With this Electric Plate Blanket you can heat stoneware and china plates to 160 F (71.1 C), which is warm enough to heat food, but not too hot to touch. And you don't need to keep the device off that lovely wooden buffet or fine oak table. It's safe. Heat resistant vinyl covers a washable, polyester-blend sleeve. The unit can heat up to ten 12" (30.5 cm) plates at once. The 56" (142.2 cm) electric cord fits into any outlet. Create that restaurant ambience right at your own table. **(I)**

PLATE-MATE

You're cruising around at a party and strike up a conversation with a business or social acquaintance. Drinking wine with one hand and holding food with another, you feel foolish when it's time to pass on your card or take down a phone number. Remember when you spilled that drink on your new suit? No more. This plastic device attaches to your plate to create a "cup" that holds the glass. You'll never make an embarrassing mess again. With Plate-Mate, you can cruise with confidence.**(C)**

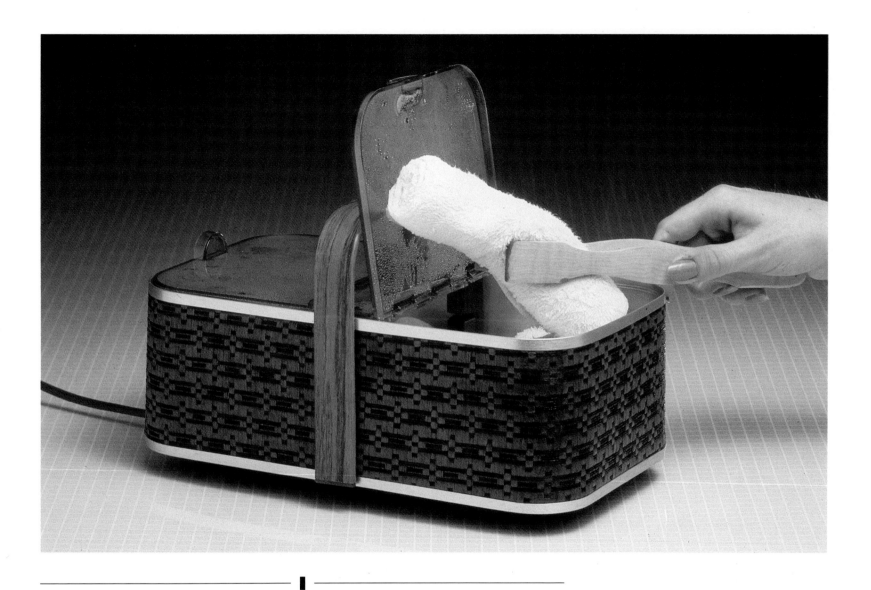

OSHIBORI HOT TOWEL BASKET

The Japanese seem to do everything right. There's something simplistically elegant about receiving a hot towel at the dinner table. The Oshibori Basket continues this two hundred-year-old tradition by heating up to fifteen small towels for you and your guests. The Oshibori preheats to 150 F (65.5 C) in three to five minutes. Hot moistened towels are ready within fifteen minutes. There's an automatic thermostat to maintain basket temperature. It also comes with a rack for steaming foods like dinner rolls, cookies, and cake. As a special feature, a dozen 12" x 12" (30.5 x 30.5 cm) blended cotton towels are included. This item uses regular electric outlets. **(I)**

The Bar

PORTABLE WINE WIZARD

Only the Rothschilds will know you've got help. With the Portable Wine Wizard, you can become that pseudo-sophisticate about whom you've always fantasized. Insult your enemies and impress your friends at parties, by expertly commenting on a wine's off year, or vintage. This ingenious, hand-held computer displays and rates dated bottles of California, French, German, and Italian wines. A second program even advises you of a bottle's aging status—whether to drink it now, let it age, or throw it away. Programmed by international wine experts, the Wine Wizard comes with a three-year battery for long term use. Voilá. **(I)**

THE THERMO-VINOMETER

Here's the sophisticated way to tell whether that homemade brew is up to snuff. If you are into moonshine, or just like to make your own wine, this Thermo-Vinometer is a must. Based on the same principle that the pros use in wine processing, this device will measure the precise alcoholic content of wines, liqueurs, and spirits. To test, simply drain a small sample of wine through the stemmed pipe by inverting it. What's left in the stem is determined by the different molecular structure of alcohol and water. To get

an alcohol reading, just look at the graduated markings which match the column height. A thermometer measures temperatures between 40 F (4.4 C) and 80 F (26.6 C). Whether you're in the back woods of the boonies, or on the sloping hills of your homegrown vineyard, the Thermo-Vinometer tells you that your homemade booze can still pack a punch. **(I)**

FOLDING INSTANT BAR

Perfect for the patio, picnics, the boat, or poolside parties. If you're on shaky ground, or there's a lot of activity and you're concerned about spillage, this Folding Instant Bar lets you drink without worry. Its 20" x 27" x 25" (51 x 68.6 x 63.5 cm) construction holds two bottles, six glasses, and ice in place, for serving and carrying beverages without spilling. There's a built-in 3 qt (2.839 l) ice bucket and bottle holders for quarts and liters. It uses salt-resistant, steel-coated legs and a special plastic top reinforced with polyester. Six 8 oz (236.59 ml) clear, high-impact styrene cups are also included. **(I)**

WORLD'S BEST CORKSCREW

According to the New York Times, this Screwpull Deux Corkscrew is the most reliable model on the market. The clothespin-like guide fits over a bottle's top and positions it in the exact center of the cork. Then, with minimum effort, you draw up the cork by continuously rotating the screw's handle. There's no pulling involved and almost no danger of damaging, or leaving pieces of cork in the bottle, even with rare old bottles. The hand-ground point and wide coils penetrate the cork completely to provide a firm grip. **(I)**

WINEKEEPER

Your friends will know you've got style when they see this device in your bar. The Winekeeper lets you serve glasses of your favorite wines without waste or decreased flavor. If you enjoy first class wine, then you know how easy it is for air to ruin the quality of a premier vintage. Once you open it, the bottle should be consumed quickly. Keeping wine in the fridge is really second-best. But with Winekeeper you can preserve that flavor. The unit creates an airtight seal around the inside of the bottle neck. As the wine is forced out under low pressure, nitrogen, not air, fills the bottle space. Thus, an opened bottle can remain on the machine for several weeks and still remain fresh. Some wine dispensing machines occasionally "pop" their stopper mechanism, allowing oxidation. There are a variety of Winekeeper sizes and quality wood finishes to accommodate home and commercial use. **(E)**

The Living Room

Gadgets

SINGING TELEPHONE

That annoying telephone ring, found in even the newer models, can get on anyone's nerves. This special unit replaces the monotonous telephone "B-R-R-R-I-N-G" with a song. Be allerted to callers by corny sounds of "La Cucuracha" or the patriot beat of "The Màrseilles". Your friends will crack up when they hear one of the eight melodies. There are also four different volume settings and the regular ring if you need it. Only some wall phones may require installation. The device connects to a modular plug and uses two 9-volt batteries that are not included. **(I)**

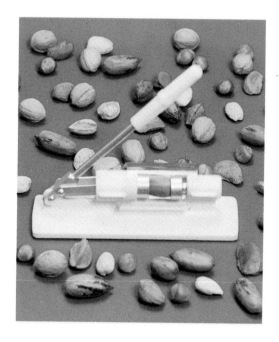

GOURMET NUTCRACKER

Oh yes . . . cracking those nuts. How many times have you or your guests struggled with the metal nutcracker only to hunt down shells and nuts that have ended up across the room? This simple device will keep your guests in their seats. The solid-cast aluminum body lets you place the nut inside a plastic covering. Also, it adjusts for different sized nuts. Just press down on the handle and start munching. A felted bottom keeps the device from scratching your good coffee table. Great for parties! **(I)**

AIR EASY POLLUTION SHIELD

The Surgeon General recently reported that cigarette smoke can even cause cancer for non-smokers. Today, smoke, smog, car fumes, and chemical pollutants make up much of the air we breathe. There's no escape. Your own home can be a refuge from some of society's pressures, but those four walls may also be housing dangerous contaminants. What can you do?

Many fans or other devices with filters get at some of the bigger irritants such as cigarette butts and large ashes. But they only filter out air they've pulled in themselves. These devices also miss the smaller pollutants which make up over ninety percent of harmful air. The Air Ease Pollution Shield reportedly gets at the smallest particles under five microns. In a 12'x 20' (3.658 x 5.944 m) area, the machine sends out a charge of negative ions which attach themselves to air pollutants. These charged particles are then attracted to a special base collector on the unit. Further away from the machine's operating area, pollutants will fall to the floor for easy vacuuming. Just wash the collector's removable filter and see what could be going into your lungs. A must for healthy living. **(I)**

SMOKEAWAY SMOKELESS ELECTRONIC ASHTRAY

Be kind to non-smokers. How many times have you walked into parties only to be over-whelmed by stagnant cigarette smoke? This ingenious device will at least pick up some of the effluent as smokers place their burning tobacco in ashtrays. The SmokeAway works silently to trap smoke and ash in its stainless steel bowl. It's similar to today's electric air cleaners in that it ionizes pollutants with a "short loop" electrostatic charge of energy. Eighty percent of the cigar and cigarette smoke burning in its base is reportedly cut out by this dark brown, 8" (20.3 cm) round device. In your home or office, this gadget will help people breathe easier. **(I)**

EFFICIENCY FIREPLACE HEAT RECYCLER

Your fireplace only gives you a portion of its heating poten-tial. Much of its heat rises up into the heavens. With this unit, you can maxi-mize that fuel-saving timber and get more for your cutting time and money. The Fireplace Recycler directs hot air from your fireplace into the room at floor level, instead of up the chimney. The distributor claims you will notice a considerable improvement—four times more heat than before. Four boiler-quality metal fins transfer heat from burning logs into air that is blown out from a bottom grate by a variable speed fan and travels up to 100 cu ft (2.8 cu m) per minute. If your fire is down to coals, the device keeps pumping out hot air for another three to four hours. The Recycler can hold up to three 6" (15.2 cm) diameter logs and fits fire-places as narrow as 23" (58.4 cm) at the back. Hinged and tapered wings can ad-just to your fireplace's width. There's a steel shovel to clear ash from between the fins. The box attaches with a metal air tube and plugs into house current. **(M)**

THE BUTTON

Add more light to your life. You're in the middle of writing an important paper when the desk light blows. There're no more bulbs left, and you can't believe it. You just changed that light last month. Doesn't it always seem that bulbs always go when you need them the most? With The Button, you can extend the life of your bulbs from sixty to one hundred times. It's not complicated. The device converts AC current to DC. This gives your lights more life. It works on any regular incan-descent bulb of up to 300 watts, except three-way bulbs. There's also a model for the popular candelabra bulbs. Put The Button on the bottom of your bulbs and screw them into place. They'll burn cooler and will give a softer, less glaring light. Of course, this will reduce the electrical output, so you may want to get a higher wattage. But they'll benefit from that same life-light extension. The Button is a solid-state microchip, based in plastic. Don't play Abe Lincoln at the fireplace. Finish that report and keep your lights burning bright. **(I)**

CHIMNEY FIRE EXTINGUISHER

Sitting in front of a fire on a wintry night can be a cozy, comforting experience but what happens when the chimney clogs up and the fire gets out of hand? You can avoid this potentially dangerous situation by having this specially designed chimney fire extinguisher on hand. Used by professional fire departments, this extinguisher puts out fires safely and quickly without water damage to the house or cracking chimney tiles. Just tear off the tape, twist the top and snap it off, then strike the exposed mixture against the cap and drop the extinguisher into your fireplace or stove. The gases released will cut off the fire's oxygen supply and smother the blaze in a moment. Be sure, for safety's sake, to familiarize yourself and your family with the use of the extinguisher. The extinguisher comes with a black matte container for storing. With this device handy, you can be sure that snuggling up to a warm fire is always a pleasant experience. **(I)**

HANDS FREE SPEAKERPHONE

You're whipping up a gourmet meal in the kitchen when that new client calls. Do you drop everything and potentially create a mess in your haste? Not any longer. This unique item lets you continue your chores or business work when the phone rings. You don't move. Just begin the conversation simply by saying hello. The device answers a telephone automatically. No need to race across the room. Carry on your conversation up to 15' (4.57 m) away so you can continue with whatever you were doing. When the conversation is finished, the unit hangs up automatically. You don't have to move. This feature is only for incoming calls. There's also a built in memory redial, group conversation button, a mute button for private conversations, and a two line capability. When you're sick of hearing that ringing bell just turn it off. A flashing Liquid Crystal Display (LCD) will tell you if a call is coming through. It's switchable for pulse or tone dialing. If you are ill, in bed, or far away from the phone, you'll appreciate this state-of-the-art system. **(I)**

INITECH 3100P PHONE ANSWERING SYSTEM

Every day, some new company comes out with an answering machine product. It's almost impossible to keep track of price value against features. However, this device catches the eye. It can save you money if you frequently check in for messages via long distance. There's no beeper. At the sound of your voice you'll know who called. If there are no messages, you don't pay for the call. Just hang up before toll charges start. The Unitech 3100P (31000 without phone) is a solid state, microprocessor-controlled system that comes with a full-featured telephone. A single key touch directs all functions automatically. There's on-hook dialing and last number redial, as well as two-way conversation recording, call screening, key touch, announcement recoding, and automatic outgoing message review. After listening to your messages, you reset the device with your own voice. **(M)**

The Bedroom

Gadgets Gadgets Gadgets Gadgets Gadgets Gadgets Gadgets Gadgets Gadgets Gadgets Gadgets Gadgets Gadgets

HEAT SENSING AUTOMATIC BLANKET

Everyone has woken up in the middle of the night, freezing, only to pile on suffocating layers of blankets which interrupt sleep later. That's why electric blankets are so popular. The problem is that they, too, can become stuffy even with a good temperature gauge. Not this special model. It adjusts its warmth to your body heat, automatically providing more heat to cold feet and other areas of the body that need it the most, while maintaining a constant temperature in other parts to avoid overheating. The wire consists of a two-conductor cable in a heat conductive sheath that spreads warmth evenly throughout the blanket. As the temperature of the wire increases, its electrical conductivity decreases so that the amount of heat generated is auto-matically controlled. Each area of the blanket maintains the level you set on the adjustable comfort control. Like to tuck and fold your covers? You won't be creating an extra "hot" spot with this comforter. The comfort controls auto-matically sense and adjust to room temperature. The Bi-Nell fabric loom is woven with triple-layered yarn for strength. Machine washable. **(I)**

■
MAGNAVOX CLOCK/AUDIO/COMMUNICATIONS CENTER

Total audio and telephone control at your fingertips. Don't even get out of bed. The alarm clock will wake you up in the morning. You can get a tone or set it to play your favorite music from the AM/FM radio or a cassette. Tired of picking up the phone? The built-in answering machine screens your calls and takes messages. Monitor the caller before you decide to answer. There's a speakerphone, automatic redialing, a mute function, and an LCD number display. The machine automatically mutes your radio or cassette when the phone is in use. **(M)**

■
INTELLIPHONE

Some of their functions are standard on a number of high-tech telephones, but for the money it seems like a valuable device. The best offering is the wake-up call in the morning with a snooze delay that gives you the exact time. The Intelliphone also holds ten frequently called numbers and automatically redials every minute—(up to ten)—if there's a busy signal. A built-in speaker lets you hear the rings so you can pick up when your party is on the line. There's a "help" button for putting that emergency call through immediately, a hold button, a bell silencer, and an LCD display that shows the number you've called. The unit even times your calls for more accurate client or household billing. It plugs into any wall jack and requires a household outlet. Works with rotary and touch-tone systems. **(I)**

■
MARSONA SOUND CONDITIONER

It's two o'clock in the morning and you can't fall asleep. Is it the faucet dripping, the wind making your house creak, or that never-ending traffic from a busy street? Whether in the country or city, we've all experienced that difficult night when the slightest noise interferes with our beauty rest. Well, here's an alternative way to get a full night's sleep without any sleeping pills. The electronic Marsona Sound Conditioner blocks out most annoying noises by producing nature's most soothing sounds to lull you off to sleep. A flowing waterfall, a pounding surf, or a mild rainstorm can be recreated by this machine to suit your exact taste. Adjustable controls let you determine the strength and volume. The unit produces what sleep experts describe as "white noise," to block out unwanted, awakening sounds. So if hubby snores a bit too loud, or those neighbors just can't seem to keep it down, this sound conditioner may be your key to a peaceful night's sleep. You won't go sleepless again. **(M)**

SAFE-ESCAPE INSTANT PORTABLE LADDER

If you live in a private home, townhouse, or brownstone, you know the fear of fire. Most small buildings don't have fire escapes and their internal sprinkler systems are risky at best. If you want something reliable to protect your family in case of emergencies, this Portable Ladder can do the job. The standard chain and rung foldout types hang loosely along the wall. When you're in a panic to get out, their shakiness may not provide a secure foothold. But this rigid steel and aluminum tubing ladder is braced by a standoff on each rung, flushing it against the building wall but keeping the rungs far enough away for a rapid descent. It unfolds and positions itself instantly, without the tangling associated with other loose metal or nylon models, so you won't lose a minute during an emergency. The Ladder can attach to window sills up to 12" (30.5 cm) deep. It has been tested to hold up to 1150 lbs (521.63 kg) so that more than one person can climb down at the same time. The reach extends up to three stories and the sturdy construction requires no assistance from below. A special top, which is included, lets you convert this ladder into a useful table until it's needed. Don't play with fire during an emergency. **(M)**

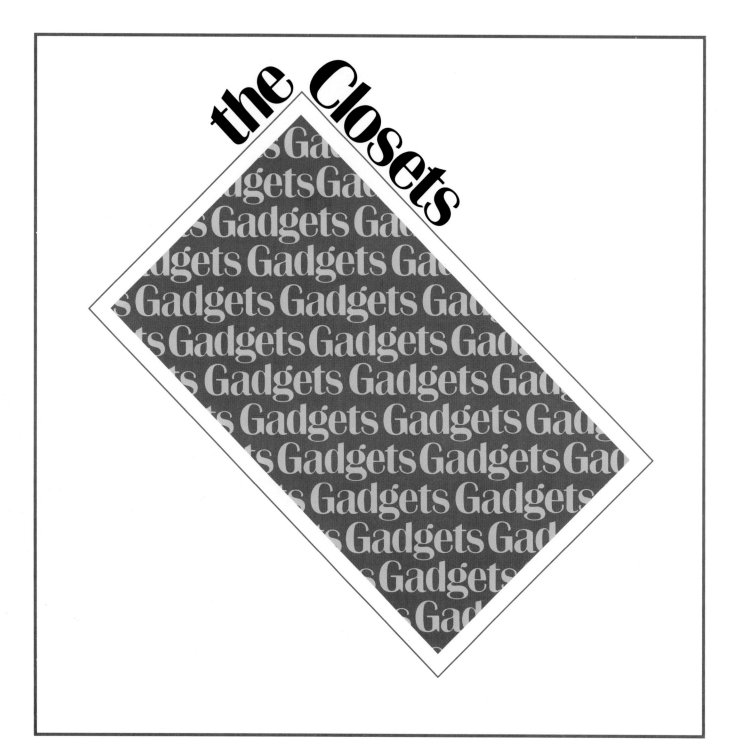

the Closets Gadgets

EXTENDABLE BELT AND TIE RACK

Tired of hunting around for ties and belts? Rushing off to work and can't find a tie that matches? Stop scrounging around on floors and hunting through yesterday's outfits? This device stores up to forty-two ties and/or belts in the space of one suit. With closet room being a premium these days, it's a great space saver. The Extendable Organizer needs only one screw and fits on any closet rod. The unit pulls out for easy selection. Your belts and ties are always wrinkle-free. If you keep your ties on one hanger, like most men, you know how functional this gadget is. **(I)**

NON-ELECTRIC DEHUMIDIFIER

Ever wonder why your clothes smell of mold or mildew even when they've only been sitting in the closet? If you live near a lake, on a boat, or in a camper where you travel through humid or wet areas, then this nonelectric dehumidifier is perfect for keeping your valuable clothes in prime condition. We've all woken up out in the country only to put on clothes that felt like they'd been left out in a storm. This device is ideal for eliminating moisture in small areas such as closets, where an expensive electric model would be a waste. The self-contained

canister holds replaceable, humidity-grabbing crystals. A lower reservoir collects excess moisture. A handy wall-mount bracket allows the unit to work in tight spaces and protect your fishing equipment, gun, stamp collection, and virtually anything else that can be ruined by too much humidity. **(C)**

ELECTRONICALLY HEATED SOCKS AND MITTENS

Need we say more? You'll always be toasty with these two timely gadgets. Keep your feet and hands warm for hours, especially when out in the snow. The socks are made of a safe thermal knit and are completely washable. They come in standard calf length gray with a red top. The mittens are black. They're made of water-repellent nylon and leather palms linked with acrylic pile. Both items are powered by size D batteries. You can use the mittens without batteries as well. **(I)**

PANTS PRESSER VALET

This solid oak Pants Presser will send you off in style. If you attend many fancy functions, you'll be noticed when you turn up with a knife-edged crease in your trousers. Just put your pants in the presser, turn on the timer, and moments later they're perfectly pressed. The distributor claims there is no chance of scorching or burning fine clothes. The Valet turns itself off automatically if you forget. It comes with a nightstand and with its own over-sized, contoured coat hanger. There's a tie rail, a clothes brush, a shoe rack, and a solid oak tray . **(I)**

THE HIDEAWAY IRONING CENTER

If you live in a small city apartment but work in an office, you know how troublesome it is to come in every morning with sharp looking clothing. An ironing board can sometimes fill an entire room, and the time it takes to put everything together doesn't help at all in today's frantic environment. In the past, people had the time and space to do their own pressing. Today, those on the go have to spend a lot of money at the dry cleaners just to keep up an appearance. Here's a convenient helper that can cut down on expenses. This compact ironing center can store all your ironing equipment in a thin upright unit. A foldable, 46″ (1.22 m) steel board stands on two adjustable legs that can be raised and lowered for individual comfort. It has a 22″ (55.9 cm) and 19½″ (49.5 cm) sleeveboard for ironing large and small sleeves. There's a built-in 110-volt outlet with a timer and safety switch that shuts off electricity automatically when the door closes. The unit also has an adjustable spotlight, a signal that indicates when the unit is operating, and storage space for your iron and any accessories. It's great for boats, dorms, or any small living space. Flush mounts for the wall, pads, and covers are included. **(E)**

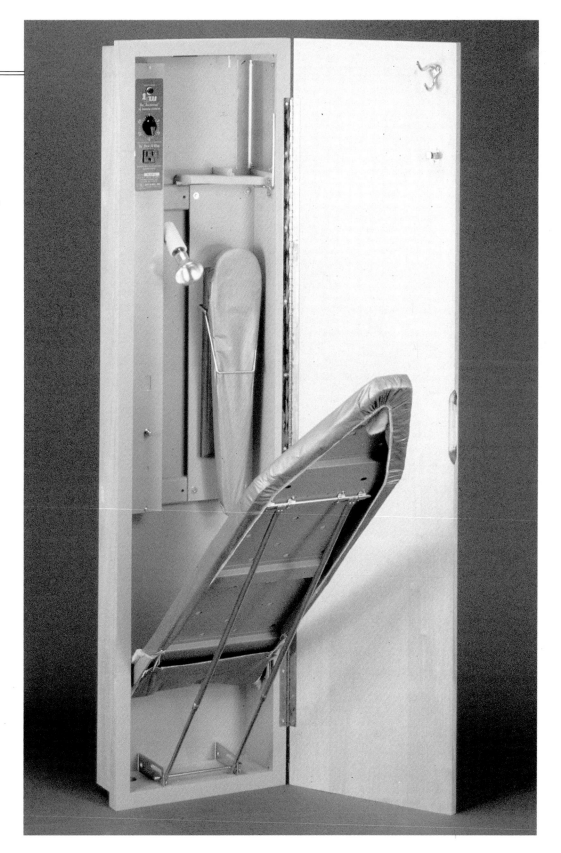

The Utility Room

STAKE-DOWN INFLATABLE HEADREST BEACH TOWEL

You're at the beach and the sun is shining. Everything is perfect. Suddenly the wind picks up and your comfortable sunbath becomes a sand shower. We've all walked out of the surf only to watch our towel blow away, or find valuables buried with mounds of sand. No longer. With this unique beach towel, you'll only get worked up by beautiful bodies. A large, yellow, terry cloth towel attaches to a 9"x 20" (22.9 cm x 51 cm) pillow that's staked down in sand to prevent it from blowing away. Most of us use personal valuables or clothing to hold down corners. But why risk sun or sand damage? Along with this unique beach towel, a companion carrying bag converts to a pillow case. The case then covers an inflatable vinyl pillow which conceals your personal items. Take that cruise down the beach without always looking over your shoulder. **(I)**

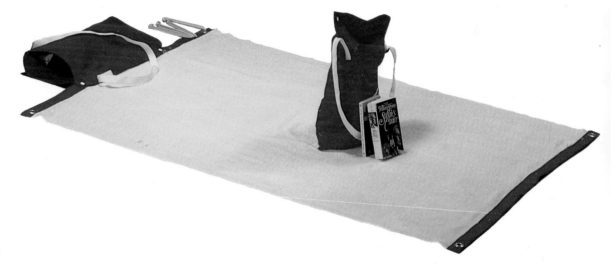

FLOATING STEREO

You're laying there on the sand, bopping to music. Suddenly the tide comes in and a wave washes all over your valuables. Or you're out in a sailboat when the wind quickly shifts. That portable radio pitches its last note overboard. To avoid these very real situations, the Floating Stereo can give you the music you want without the fear of damage from water, sun, or sand. This 200 MW auto-reverse stereo cassette player has an AM/FM stereo tuner and built-in 4-ohm speakers with a frequency response from 100-1500 Hz. Water resistant headphones can give even better listening sound from the unit, which won't sink and can withstand damage from saltwater, chlorine, and even sand. Its perfect for the pool or beach. A built-in, 4.5-volt, high-beam flashlight also provides illumination. **(M)**

AUTOMATIC PET WATERING SYSTEM

How many vacations have you cancelled or cut short because no one could check up on the dog? There are a number of automatic dry food feeders on the market today, but admit it, you've had nightmares of coming home and finding your loving animal dehydrated to the point of no return. If you're the typical neurotic pet owner who worries about your pet's water spilling or evaporating while you're gone, then this system may relieve your anxiety. Nearly 3 qts (2.84 l) of water are freshened as your pet requires. Just connect the hose to an outdoor faucet (this device is not for city dwellers) and a float-operated valve prevents overflow or recirculation. Three stakes anchor the device to the ground to prevent spills. No more morbid animal fantasies during that long summer weekend, please. **(I)**

ELECTRONIC FLEA COLLAR

Chances are that your dog or cat has had fleas or ticks at one point. So you know how annoying it can be to keep their bodies free from the pests. Flea collars help but in most cases, if they get wet their effectiveness soon disappears. Well, here's another high-tech invention that will safely bring your dog into state-of-the-art living—the Electronic Flea Collar. It uses ultrasound to drive fleas and ticks away. The unit surrounds your pet with a field of safe, inaudible, high-frequency sound waves using a pulsating, modulated circuit. There are no chemicals or positions required. And when the unit gets wet, the automatic circuitry shuts off. It's completely waterproof. Testing proved this microtech unit 100 percent safe for your pet. Complete with a durable nylon collar and long-life batteries. **(I)**

MAGNETIC WINDOW CLEANER

Do you live in a tall building or have more than a one-story home? Then you know how tough it is to clean the outside windows. Shy of risking our lives or paying an expensive professional, many of us look out through dirt and grime. Well, this double-padded magnetic device may brighten your day. Barium-ferrite ceramic magnets create 20 lbs (9.1 kg) of pull, holding two parallel pads together through the glass. Move the inside cleaning pad and the outside one cleans simultaneously. A safety line prevents separation. The device uses a standard glass cleaner. Let the sunshine in. **(I)**

SURVIVOR 15-FUNCTION TOOL

Can't get out of the rough? There are a number of these all-inclusive tools, but this one seems to have more sophisticated applications. The hardened steel blade reportedly works as a saw, wrench, can opener, knife, bottle opener, chisel, wire stripper, compass, and protractor. There's a built-in magnifying glass for animal and plant study, and it even starts campfires if you've forgotten the matches. The plastic handle becomes a ruler. It contains flip-out scissors and a Phillips screwdriver. There are even Morse code signals inscribed on the blade to use as a reflector if you're really in trouble. **(I)**

ARIA LIGHT SOCKET FAN

Cool off quickly! Don't run up big electric bills by air-conditioning an entire room. Just plug this fan into any light socket and cool air gets directed to exactly where you want it. Whether you use it when you're at your desk, or lying in bed, the Aria Socket Fan is excellent for small corners or in cooking areas where large, noisy fans are not desirable. Go for the flow. **(I)**

LONG BURNING CANDLE

As municipal power needs continue to rise, the prospect of blackouts is very real. Flashlights help, but sometimes a storm or power outage can take days to fix. You'll be replacing batteries all the time. Relax. This candle will burn for almost three days if necessary, so that you can at least function without panic. It's formed by compressing paraffin under 1,600 lbs (726 kg) of pressure. This helpful candle won't smoke or drip, and it won't soften in the summer heat. Clean and even-burning, it emits a pleasant vanilla scent. **(C)**

COMPUTEMP 3 TEMPERATURE/CLOCK

If you work on the land, or are concerned about temperature fluctuations for a variety of reasons, this handy gadget may help out. The Computemp 3 is a precision instrument that accurately reports indoor and outdoor temperatures and their time of day by using a bright LCD display. A special remote-wired sensor lets you monitor outdoor air, soil, or water temperatures. Worried about animals or pipes freezing? Pre-set levels for extremes to sound an alarm if they're passed. A twenty-four-hour memory stores the day's high and low readings and the times they occurred. It can also become a standard alarm clock with a snooze setting. Know your environment. **(I)**

PEST-PRUFF II

Put off those pests. You'll send roaches and rodents packing with this state-of-the-art pest control device. It's revolutionizing the extermination business. No need to hire expensive professionals to get rid of unwanted guests. You can't sense it and neither can your pets. But once this electronic pest chaser starts working, mice, rats, and roaches will checkout fast. The special sound waves create an unpleasant ambience for your uninvited company. They'll get the hint quickly. It covers up to 2500 cu ft (71 cu m)—anywhere there's a 110-volt socket—and works best on surfaces like hardwood floors and tiled kitchens that don't absorb the sound. It's completely safe and sanitary since there are no messy traps. With the Pest-Pruff II unit, you can put away those toxic poisons. **(I)**

ELECTROSONIC JEWELRY CLEANER

Don't waste money at the jeweler's. It's hard enough to pay for the sparklers. Why spend unnecessarily to have them cleaned? The Electrosonic Jewelry Cleaner uses gentle, low-frequency sonic waves to put the luster back into your precious metals and stones. It's the same process many jewelers use themselves. The device handles gemstones, gold, silver, fashion jewelry, and even pearls. Economical, it comes complete with a non-toxic, non-oxidizing jewel and pearl cleaning solution, as well as a touch-up brush, polishing cloth, and six page jewelry care guide. The distributor says that the sculpted jewel box design enhances your bedroom or bath decor, but I'd keep it in the closet until the job needs to get done. **(I)**

THE GABOT DOUBLE UMBRELLA

You're out for an evening with your date, dressed to the hilt. Rain was predicted, but only one of you has an umbrella. How many times have you come home dripping wet on one side because there wasn't enough room? If the thought of ruining that beautiful silk outfit disturbs you, then purchasing this double umbrella may provide sheltering thoughts. This 53" x

44" (134.6 x 111.8 cm) nylon canopy protects two or more people from even the heaviest rainstorms. It's really two umbrellas fused together. Sixteen sturdy chrome-plated steel ribs operate on two 27" (68.6 cm) steel shafts. A spring mechanism automatically opens and closes the umbrella. **(I)**

RETRACTABLE DOG LEASH

Tired of getting a sore arm every time you take your Siberian Husky out for a walk? This gadget may ease the pain. Elderly people have particular difficulty containing excitable pets that sometimes dart ahead on a whim. Or, if you are jogging with your animal, matching speeds can interfere with the entire workout: Yes, fixed-length leashes severely restrict a dog's freedom. But with this retractable device, you can extend the leash up to 487.7 cm and retain full control with the touch of a button. Press the release button into the comfortable handpiece and you allow more space for your pet. Just stop the line extension at will. The handpiece is made of impact-resistant plastic. Two sizes accommodate different dog weights. **(I)**

MINI-VAC

Blowing a tube used to be the electronic hobbyists' worst enemy. Today, dirt is the number one bugaboo. Sophisticated electronic and high-tech equipment now have few moving parts. But dirt and dust can easily jam up the works by inhibiting microprocessors and state-of-the-art circuitry. Wiping and dusting hardly help because of tight construction. Using this mini-vacuum can keep your equipment at top of the line form by getting in hard-to-reach areas. It also works as a blower to remove dust where vacuuming is impractical. The unit was originally created for cleaning fine photographic equipment. So it comes with a first quality lens brush that is ideal for cameras. But Mini-Vac will also help clean stereos, VHF equipment, computers, typewriters, and other modern electronic gear. It uses an easy-to-empty bag, two fine brush nozzles, and two directional wands. **(I)**

URINE KLEEN

Another must for your pet "fido" and "tabby." Chances are, on more than one occasion, your dog or cat has mistaken your beautiful oriental rug for the litter box or backyard. Particularly with cats, once they get started on a spot, they mistakenly continue with their bathroom habits. The smell reminds them where to go. With this Urine Kleen, you will stop that unpleasant odor in its tracks. The special formula instantly neutralizes any type of urine odor on any surface. Just spray it on and rub thoroughly. This non-toxic formula is reportedly so safe that it can even be sprayed directly on your pet. **(C)**

DOUBLE BUFFER ELECTRIC SHOE POLISHER

Wasn't it grandpa who once said he could always tell a person by their shoes? If you work for a conglomerate, or just like to look your best everyday, you know how important polished shoes are to one's appearance. Most people seem to wait until after they're completely dressed before shining their shoes. Don't you get sick of bending, stooping, and kneeling just to get that luster? This Electric Shoe Polisher provides a quick, professional quality shine while you remain standing. A carry around handle contains the controls, so you stay on your feet. Avoid getting messy polish on your hands and fine clothes while you buff. Two natural lamb's wool buffers spin at 1500 RPM to buff and shine either light or dark shoes, with or without shoe polish. A rubber-tipped bottom provides stability and prevents scratching. **(M)**

MINIATURE FOLDING UMBRELLA

How many umbrellas did you lose during the rainy season? Especially if you live in a city, leaving umbrellas at different locations is always a common occurance. It's gotten to the point that when it starts to rain, people pay five dollars for a cheap, poorly constructed umbrella on the street. Either through breakage or absentmindedness, they know full well it will be gone by morning. So stop adding to restaurant lost and found racks. This Miniature Umbrella collapses to a flat 1¼"x 8¼"x 2¼" (3.17 x 20.95 x 5.71 cm), two-thirds the size of conventional folding models. At 20 oz (567 g) you can stick it back into your pocketbook or briefcase without even thinking. When it rains a few days later, you'll be prepared. Don't keep an umbrella off your person because it's too big. This unit comes in a black nylon covering that has double-stitched seams for strength and head-sealed edges that resist wear and fraying. The canopy spreads 34" (86.4 cm) across and 8½" (21.6 cm) deep. Ribs are designed to give during heavy wind so that there's no turning inside out. The shaft extends 20" (51 cm). Stop spending money on new umbrellas every time it rains. This is the only umbrella you'll ever need, and you'll never be caught in the rain. **(I)**

XTRALITE

Can't see too well in that musty attic? Did the people who used to own the house forget to wire a closet or crawl space you need? No need to spend money or time on electrical installations. This simple, portable light will provide the illumination you need to get any job done. It can be fastened anywhere and uses four AA batteries with a manual on/off switch. There's also a built-in timer that shuts off after 30 seconds. Stop stumbling around in the dark. **(I)**

THE CURRENCY EXCHANGER BILLFOLD

With the fluctuations in international monetary markets these days, this gadget is almost a necessity for traveling overseas. The leather case is large enough to hold your passport and has ample compartments for traveler's checks and credit cards. But the most important feature is the built-in compact calculator. It will help you convert cash/money transactions in any country so that you know exactly what your dollar is worth. The calculator is held in place magnetically, detaches for easy use. The Currency Exchange Billfold comes in various colors. **(I)**

PET WASHER

Dogs have a bad habit of rolling around in their playmates' excrement. Yes, we've all come home to find "fido" filling our house with a horrible smell. The thought of washing that day of play away is also not very appetizing. Here's a simple gadget that can make the job much easier. Shaped like a bar of soap, the pet washer head fits easily in your hand. It's a water, shampoo, and grooming brush all in one. The device gives you one free hand to keep your pet still. The bristle brush loosens dirt and removes fleas and ticks as it lifts the outer and inner layers of hair. The shampoo and water get right down to the skin, even when the brush is held upside down. You can wash your dog's underside without trouble. The Pet Washer can also be used for applying medication to a limited area. **(I)**

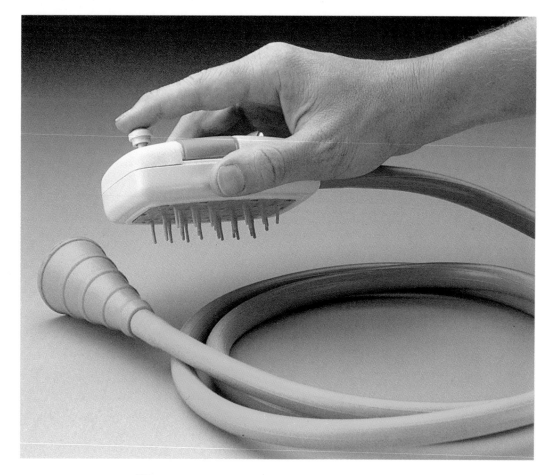

The Playroom And The Den

=58=

THE 360° PANORAMIC CAMERA

Have you ever been in a beautiful location and thought of how exciting a complete 360 degree view would look as a picture? Now it's possible to get that entire panorama without being a professional. This unique model is, reportedly, the only camera that allows you to record a complete viewpoint using regular 35mm film. The New York Times describes it as the "ultimate wide-angle camera." Take pictures of large groups, dramatic landscapes, and architectural photographs for as many as eight camera rotations in a single shot. The patented, ribbon-spring, fluid-clutch motor has no gears, eliminating vibrations. To take the picture, you press an activator button. The spring-wound motor rotates the fixed-focus, wide-angle lens for exposures equivalent of one-fortieth and one two-hundredth of a second. The camera produces up to eight 360 degree pictures per 36-exposure roll of film. An F3.5 lens stops down to F22. There's a split leveler for adjusting the camera on the tripod. **(E)**

"MONTY"— COMPUTER SCRABBLE MASTER

Improve your vocabulary while having fun. Play against "Monty," the world's only hand held Scrabble computer. He has a vocabulary of up to 12,000 words that can be expanded up to 44,000 with add-on microchips from the Official Scrabble Player's Dictionary. "Monty" creates multiple word combinations, uses bonus points, and challenges incorrect entries. He can play against three human competitors with four different skill levels at the same time. "Monty" assigns tiles, calculates scores for player names, and handles other necessary scrabble functions. He even prints congratulatory remarks on his screen, such as "good play," while performing a few bars from the 1812 Overture. If you're stuck, "Monty" provides hints by showing you his solutions. He's even small enough to hold. Check the skill level you want when ordering "Monty." **(M)**

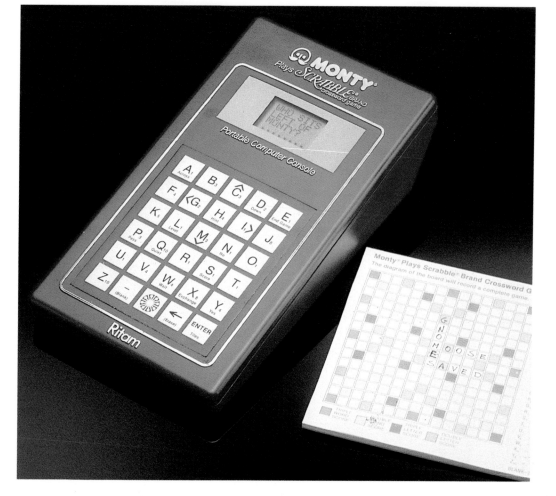

COMPUTERIZED BRIDGE SCORECARD

If you're one of those players that just hates to keep score, this item may lend a hand. Reportedly endorsed by World Champion Bridge Master Charles Goren, this electronic bridge scorekeeper tracks all bids, doubles, honors, penalties, and bonuses. It indicates vulnerability, in both game and rubber points, and then at the touch of a button displays scores in LCD numbers. Two 3-volt alkaline batteries last for hours of playing time. **(I)**

REMOTE CONTROLLER FOR VHF/UHF

No need to buy a new television just to get that remote control unit. This device will upgrade your television. If you've been dying to tune out those commercials, but haven't had the dough to do the dirty deed, this cordless, infrared remote controller uses advanced microprocessor technology to put all VHF and UHF channels at your control. It's hand held and comes with a lighted, digital channel display box. There's also a model for cable connections. The model listed uses Channel 3, but there's one that works with Channel 12 as well. Check with your cable operator before ordering. **(M)**

VIDEO ORGANIZER

Having trouble finding shelf space to house your newly acquired videocassette collection? You're not alone. All across the country, people are grappling with this simple but troublesome problem. The difficulty is that furniture and home entertainment manufacturers are only now beginning to think about spacial needs for the high-tech age. Videocassettes aren't beautiful enough to want them on display. At the same time, they're an off size, so many shelves can't hold a lot of them neatly. In the interim, this Video Organizer can help out. The Organizer slips over any interior door to provide eight useful 18" (45.7 cm) wide, 5" (12.7 cm) deep shelves. There's nothing to install. Just connect the two sections and use the bracket to hang the unit on your door. You can also mount the shelves on the wall for side-by-side storage. Its dimensions run 18"x 72"x 5" (45.7 x 182.9 x 12.7 cm). Forget fumbling around to find your favorite movie. The Organizer also stacks paperback books as well, another unsightly storage problem. **(I)**

REMOTE CONTROL SEDUCTION

The future is now. Your entire house can be controlled by the touch of a button. Heat, lights, electronic lock systems, automatic sprinklers, and much more can be manipulated by this state-of-the-art system. At your beck and call, a command console sends signals throughout the wiring of your home to turn on module-connected appliances and amenities. Want the music up and the lights dimmed? Don't break that special moment by getting up. A separate ultrasonic remote lets you operate the console from up to thirty feet away. The system can control up to sixteen devices but you can add another console if you want to double the unit's capacity. There's also a timer that can be purchased to give you more flexibility when you're away from home. There's also a Telephone Responder to get things going at the sound of your voice. This extra feature is great if you have a winter cabin or a home in brush-fire country. At the sound of your voice, needed heat can be turned on to prevent pipes from freezing, or an automatic sprinkler system will engage to guard against fire. The basic Control Console **(I)** gives you control of up to sixteen different modules. The Remote **(C)** spans up to 30 feet. A thirty-two Event Clock Timer **(I)** lets you manipulate eight modules with up to two on and two off commands to each. It also acts as a command base, plus sleep and security extras. By calling your home and entering a special code with the Telephone Responder **(I)**, you control any eight of your various devices. Modules must be purchased separately for lamps, wall switches, and appliances—all **(C)**. A thermostat module is in the **(I)** category. Take control of your environment with the simple touch of a button.

THE TALKING COMPUTER BRIDGE PLAYER

Lonely, or maybe you need practice for your Thursday night partners? This machine lets you play a complete game of bridge without anyone else. Reportedly designed by a top-rated bridge master, it realistically plays one, two, or three bridge hands of real and practice games at various skill levels, from beginning to master. In addition, it can play four hands for instruction. The Talking Bridge Player announces all plays and bids in a human-like voice while displaying the same information on its LCD numbered screen. Using optical scanning, the machine reads the cards. It combines standard American bidding with European systems and uses well-known bidding conventions: Stayman, Blackwood, Gerber, Baron, Jacoby Transfers, and others. The computer indicates vulnerability and dealer positions, rejects illegal bids, doubles and redoubles, and records the initial contract and number of tricks made or set. It comes with three felt playing boards and two decks of coded playing cards. **(E)**

CHESS KING POCKET MICRO

Whether you're practicing for the internationals, or you just like a good challenge, this Chess King Pocket Micro lets you play at your own level. The sophisticated technology allows you to play in any four skill levels—novice, beginner, intermediate, or expert. The computer performs special moves, including castling and pawn promotion. If you think you're losing, switch sides and watch what the computer does to rally. It's 8" (20.3 cm) long when folded and makes a good traveling companion with which to pass the time. **(I)**

THE VOICE DEACTIVATED ALARM CLOCK

State-of-the-art sleeping. This alarm clock stops beeping at the sound of your voice, or any other noise above fifty-six decibels. A small microphone detects sudden noises and shuts the alarm off for four minutes. You can ease back into sleep before the beeping resumes, getting louder gradually for a pleasant wake-up. You can reset the alarm for up to forty-minute cycles. It's deactivated manually by pressing a bar on top. Luminescent hands make seeing the time easy in the dark. **(I)**

REMOTE CONTROL WATCH

It looks like a standard quartz watch, but behind the LCD digital readout is a gadget freak's delight. Just touch a button and you can turn on lights, stereos, and many other household electronic devices. Just plug either of the two receiver inputs into any electric device under 300 watts. Through two channels, a light emitting diode on the watch sends out a beam of invisible infrared light. Presto! Appliances jump on. All you need is a "line of sight" between the watch transmitter and the receiver. It works up to 20' (61 cm) but has been reported effective as high as 40' (12.2 m). This unique watch also contains a twenty-four hour alarm, an hourly chime, and a twelve-hour stop watch. The manufacturer says it's water resistant up to 60' (18.29 m) below the surface. The Remote Control Watch costs only $9.00, but there's a catch. The distributor wants to sell its own brand of cassette tapes. So add another $24.00 for ten, money-back-guaranteed, ninety-minute blank cassettes. **(I)**

CITIZEN CHRONOGRAPH/STOPWATCH

There are countless stop-watch models around these days. But this unit might catch your eye if you race frequently or need to be reminded of appointments. The manufacturer has taken the high-tech dashboard from the "Z" cars and turned it into a watch. Two bright LCD displays give you the time and date. It can also measure speed as a stopwatch and lap timer, in minutes, seconds, and even one thousandths of a second. There's a colored graphic timer to tell you elapsed time in red, green, and yellow. So you'll go from zero to sixty in a blaze of colors. The built-in alarm and chime alert warn the wearer of appointments, or signal the end of a countdown. It's available in metallic or high-tech black. **(M)**

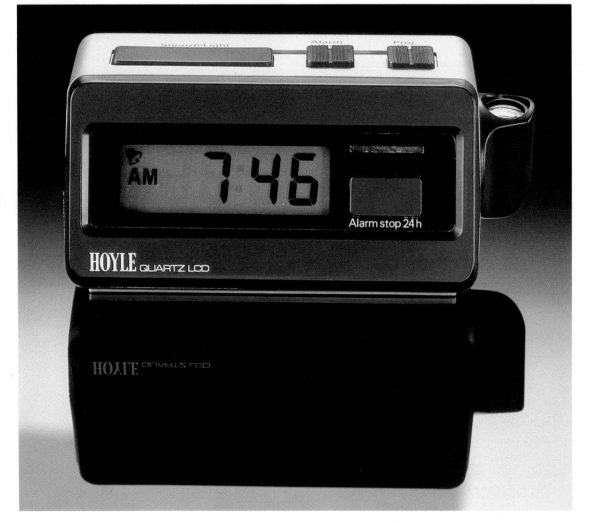

THE CEILING PROJECTOR CLOCK

Another luxury for your bedroom. This unique Quartz movement alarm clock lets you check the time in the middle of the night while lying down. If you have to feed a newborn baby or need to take medicine at a certain hour, now there's no need to stumble around and wake up your mate to check the time. A patented illuminator lens casts large, instantly discernible numbers on to the ceiling. During the day, there's a lighted LCD display. The 4.5-volt projector lamp uses standard current. The LCD display and a built-in alarm with a special snooze setting use batteries. They're included with the clock. **(I)**

COMPUTERIZED HOME METEORLOGICAL STATION

Now you can really be part of your environment. If you or the kids are weather freaks, this state-of-the-art unit will keep you occupied for hours. Its special sensors let you monitor ten separate meteorological conditions. No need to rely on governmental services that might be miles away. This unit gathers, displays, and stores information on weather conditions that can change quickly. If you live out in the woods or up in the mountains, you know how unpredictable the weather can be. Measure the humidity with a synthetic hygrometer that works even in sub-freezing temperatures. The barometer works at altitudes of up to ten thousand feet. There's a wind gauge that measures up to 150 miles per hour and can withstand violent storms up to 250 mph! A self-emptying rain gauge measures up to 99.99" (253.97 cm). Indoor and outdoor temperatures are monitored from -127 to 127 F (-88.3 to 52.7 C). Maximum and minimum outside temperatures and barometric pressures are recorded and stored along with maximum wind gusts and rainfall accumulation, so you can track patterns as well. The microprocessor computes wind chill, degree days heating, and degree days cooling. For controls, an auto-select gives four-second readouts of each function in sequence, plus time and date. This sophisticated device uses regular household current. There's even a battery back-up to protect memory during a power failure. The controls mount on the wall and the rooftop unit monitors from above. **(VE)**

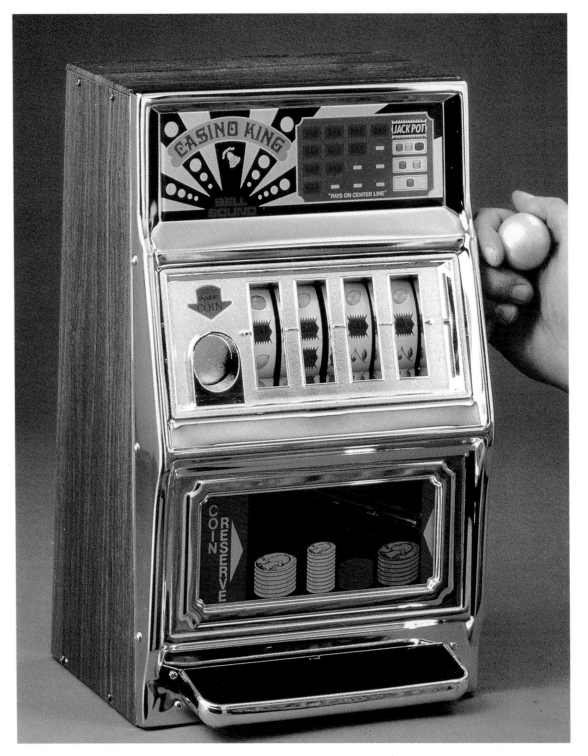

100 YEAR NIGHT LIGHT

What more could you ask for, a night light that burns for one hundred years...continuously if necessary. You'll never have to remember to flick on that switch in your child's bathroom. The distributor claims the device uses half as much current as regular night-lights. **(C)**

LAS VEGAS ONE-ARMED BANDIT

Almost everyone likes to gamble. Well, now you can collect all that money you've loaned friends and acquaintances over the years. Just invite them over to your house and show off this gadget. Before you know it, they'll be stuffing the slots with pennies, nickels, dimes, quarters, and even half dollars. You can also play the One-Armed Bandit without coins. Seduce your friends into playing. If they accidentally hit, give them their money back but nothing more. Say it's the kids' lunch money. If they lose, commiserate. But when they leave, push the release button in the back and you'll never hunt for laundry change again. **(M)**

ALPHA 8 TRANSLATOR

If you can't get past "ou est le Louvre?" then this device better accompany you on your travels. More and more Americans are going overseas these days due to the high rate of our dollar. Unfortunately, our school systems are lax in encouraging the study of foreign languages. Some Europeans speak four different languages. They think we Americans are ignorant or cultural imperialists. Many won't even answer questions unless you use their native tongue. If you are tired of feeling foolish when asking questions, then take Alpha 8 along for the ride. At the touch of a button, any one of three separate dictionaries gives you an instant English translation of words in French, Spanish, and German. Want to ask a question in German? Just enter the English words and presto!—you're on your way to that Gasthaus beer. Each device stores up to sixteen commonly used words in its memory. For foreign language students, the units expand your vocabulary. Over four hundred words of each language are in memory and appear with grammatical explanations such as gender, plural forms, irregular verbs, and verbs with prepositions. There are some American expressions as well. There's also a practice key which calls up words at random, just to test your skill. !t comes with a four-function calculator. Each language must be purchased separately. **(I)**

TELEPHONE HEARING AMPLIFIER

With today's deregulation of long distance lines, telephone connections are sometimes fuzzy at best. If you have a hearing problem, it's even worse. Well, stop straining to hear your friends and loved ones. With this in-line telephone amplifier, they'll sound just right. Plug the modular clip from your receiver into the unit's back. Then plug the amplifier lead into your handset. There are no batteries needed. The on/off switch and power slide lever give you full control without affecting volume on the other end of the line. A Velcro pad creates a convenient attachment to your phone base. It doesn't work with cordless or trimline phones. **(I)**

CORDLESS STEREO HEADPHONES

Are you sick of hearing the kids blasting the stereo? Or are you doing chores and want to listen to music without waking the whole house? With these wireless stereo headphones, the enjoyment of great stereo music can be had up to 35' (10.67 m) away from your high fidelity system. The unit's infrared stereo transmitter plugs into your receiver's headphone jack, using regular wall current. The device then sends the stereo signals to a sensor on top of the cordless headphones. It's music to your ears as you go about your business, or just lie there relaxing. **(I)**

HOME VIDEO PRINTER

Now you can isolate images from a video screen right in your own home. If your company frequently makes information videos and sales updates for local office viewing, you may occasionally need to capture a shot. Rather than edit or freeze the frame, this video printer gives you black and white prints directly from the built-in video port of your television, VCR, or personal computer monitor. If you are worried about break-ins in your small store, just hook this device up to a video security camera. Within fifteen seconds you can get a record of suspicious patrons or delivery people. Copy stock reports, recipes, or other information displayed on the screen. The prints are almost 4"x 4" (10.2 x 10.2 cm), and the device can make up to two hundred of them from the included 82½' (25.16 m) roll of thermo-sensitive paper. They come in shades of white, gray, and black. Make multiple copies at the touch of a button. It uses standard RCA jacks and regular wall current. There's also a wired, remote control switch. **(E)**

VER-BOT VOICE ACTIVATED ROBOT

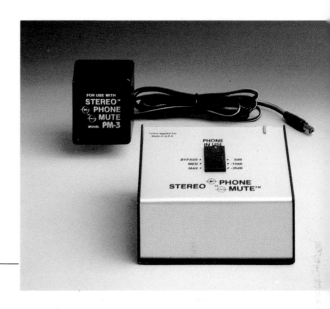

Robotic technology is still crude for consumer use, but this unit will still give you hours of fun. Verbot recognizes voice commands and takes action. Using a wireless remote control microphone, you can send him eight different commands. Tell him to: "move forward," "stop," "pick up (an object)," "carry it to me," and others. Your friends will love it when this guy gets going. If you want a sidekick to play the fool, there's another smaller robot...Ding-Bot. Let him go in crowds or parties. He bangs into objects, shakes his head, chatters to himself, and then moves on to the next crack-up. **(I)**

PHONE ACTIVATED STEREO SILENCER

You're a freelancer, so chances are the music is always going while you work at home. But when clients call, sometimes you don't have a chance to lower it. If you've felt uncomfortable talking to that stiff corporate president while "Iron Butterfly" blasts in the background, then this Stereo Silencer may help maintain your business image. This ingenious device lowers your stereo's volume automatically when the phone rings or when you pick up the receiver to make a call. As soon as you hang up, the volume rises back to its original setting. Simply plug this device into your amplifier and phone jacks. Reportedly, it can not interfere with the music quality because it's not connected to the stereo circuits. The gadget uses infrared light within the circuit board, instead of wiring, to activate the sound adjustments. Your speakers are protected from sudden jolts of power because sound fades in and out. You decide if you want the volume cut in half, or completely faded. It can also be used with headphones, remote speakers, speakerphones, cordless phones, and component televisions. It won't interfere with tape recordings so you can continue making that favorite cassette. Keep those billings flowing while you bop to your favorite beat. **(I)**

HOLMES AIR ULTRASONIC HUMIDIFIER

Humidifiers are nothing new. But this state-of-the-art device seems to get the job done without the difficulties. Most humidifiers on the market sound so loud you'd think their purpose would be to clean out a room. Then there's the messy job of cleaning and maintenance. Standard models generally use fiber belts and sponges that need to be replaced. Well, this device is reportedly so quiet that it won't wake you or disturb a TV or stereo. The Holmes Humidifier uses silent, ultrasonic sound vibrations to generate a cool mist so fine that it's easily absorbed by the air. Just set the dial to determine the moisture level you prefer. The removable tank is filled at any faucet and the reservoir level can be checked at a glance. It shuts off automatically when empty and can run up to sixteen hours without refilling. One unit is large enough for 1500 sq ft (139.35 sq m). It makes sound sense. **(M)**

The Exercise Room

TACHIKAWA FULL BODY MASSAGE MACHINE

The ultimate in electric massage. Reportedly, this is the only unit that actually simulates a hand massage over your entire body. Designed by orthopedic surgeons and physical therapists, eight specially contoured rubber rollers move beneath the surface in a slow, vigorous, undulating pattern. Up and down the entire table, you get completely massaged every forty-five seconds to help relax the neck, shoulders, back, buttocks, thighs, and calves. Simulated finger and hand movements provide therapeutic pressure to limber up still muscles, relieve stress, and improve circulation. The curved roller track accomodates varying widths of vertebrae, flexing the spinal column and adjacent tissue. You can target the desired area with a full, upper, or lower body only massage. There's a pad to tone down the rollers for reduced action. The unit's legs fold up for convenient storage. After a stressful day, you'll never leave the machine. **(VE)**

DIGITAL JOG AND WALK PEDOMETER

Want to set up a specific jogging or sprinting exercise plan? If you're considering serious training, this digital jog and walk pedometer lets you completely monitor your efforts. Total distance, stride length, and how many steps you take over a set area can be measured for maximum exercise efficiency. Just clip it to your waistband and you're off and running. **(I)**

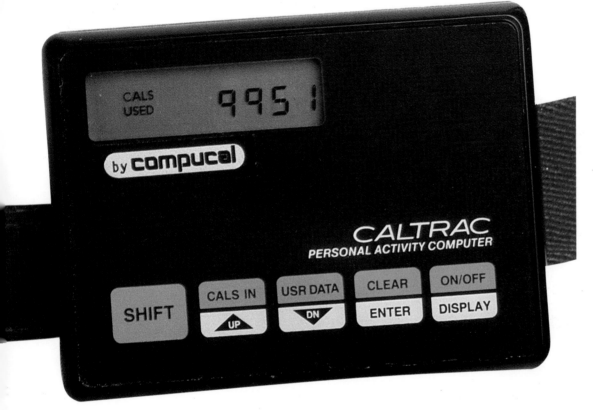

PEDIO MASSAGER

With today's fast-paced, changing economy, many people pound the pavement seeking new opportunities. But a hectic lifestyle can also take a toll on tired feet. For some, a calming, daily foot massage may be a cheaper solution than that high priced "shrink." To help you relax, this Pedio unit's "massage finger" gets at tired, aching muscles by stimulating selected reflex zones recognized for their ability to rejuvenate and improve bodily functions. It's powerful enough to massage feet even with shoes on. Luxury European hotels are reportedly using this unit to pamper their important guests. The Pedio Massager can also be used for massaging other parts of the body like the lower back, upper legs, arms, and calves. If the world feels a little too heavy today, think about giving your feet some rest and relaxation. (I)

PERSONAL CALORIE MONITOR/COMPUTER

If you're serious about weight control, or are currently training for a sport, then getting this state-of-the-art device is food for thought. Reportedly proven on target plus or minus five percent over a twenty-four-hour period, the unit gauges the calories you burn by resting, sleeping, and exercising. The device then subtracts this figure after calculating your daily food intake, so you know where you really stand. First, the computer's memory stores your personal data, including height, weight, sex, and age. With this information, the machine calculates a figure for activities like sleeping and resting, which can total up to 75 percent of the calories you burn each day. Then, using an enclosed guide covering over one thousand foods and beverages, you input the amount of food calories consumed. Calories used up by walking or exercising are measured by an accelerometer that clips on to your belt. Its tiny sensor measures the intensity of your movements and then determines their caloric value. An activity monitor even lets you judge the efficiency of specific exercises. Finally, the unit subtracts the total calories used up in one day. (I)

RUN ALERT

Another good exercise aid. This helpful device measures the quality of your running. It can help guide you to improve your form and prevent any injuries. Running too hard is a common problem for novice sprinters. Most professionals strike the ground with a force only two and a half times their body weight. Casual runners often take up to five times their weight. By clipping Run Alert on to your waistband, you can guard against painful injuries to the foot, knee, leg, hip, and back. It's like having a trainer right there. Set the adjustable control to any of ten impact settings. If you exceed it, the device will beep to let you know. As your form improves, you will get less beeps and should be running longer and more efficiently. The folks at the office will be in shock. **(I)**

BENNETT'S BEND TENNIS RACQUET

A patented 19" (48.3 cm) curved handle reduces the muscular stress which causes tennis elbow and other injuries. Reportedly, this racquet will increase the power of your stroke by as much as thirty percent, while providing a more relaxed and natural grip. Designed to fit the natural curve of a closed hand, the racket's stroking angle is better aligned with your forearm's axis to minimize the tension from a bent wrist. The result is a more efficient, powerful stroke. Shock is more evenly absorbed by the wrist and forearm muscles to reduce stress. The distributor claims that for the first time, forehand and backhand shots can be made without readjusting your grip. Comes with a mid-sized 10¼" x 13" (26 x 33 cm) head. Available in two sizes strung or unstrung. Specify. **(M)**

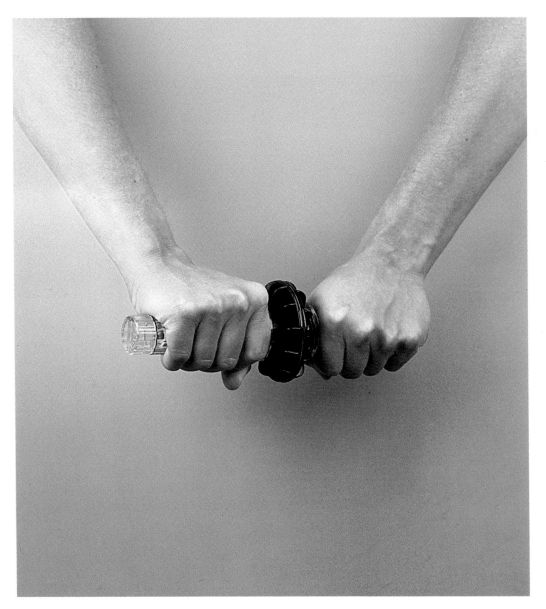

ACCU-VIBE MASSAGER

Massage those sore, hard-to-reach muscles. If you have a painful muscle spasm or ache in the middle of your back, then this special, angled massager can reach it with relief. It has a right angled, "elbow" handle, so your back, shoulders, lower back, and upper arms quickly receive penetrating relaxation. An adjustable handle control sets vibration level from four protruding fingers. Direct the vibrating pressure to the precise point and level you need. It's 12" (30.48 cm) long and uses household current. (I)

GRIP EXERCISER

Want to strengthen your grip for tennis, golf, baseball or other sports? Use this Grip Exerciser just a few minutes each day and watch your game improve. This handy device will build muscle in your wrists, hands and forearms giving you more power, control, and accuracy for just about any sport. Easy to use, just hold the exerciser in both hands and rotate the handles in opposite directions. A control knob at the end of one handle lets you adjust the tension for different levels of difficulty. This model is made of high-impact plastic, is about 10" (25 cm) long and weighs a mere 10 ozs. (311 g). After a few weeks with the Grip Exerciser, your favorite sport is a breeze. (I)

PORTABLE HEART WINDOW

This portable device can help you excel in today's physical fitness race. If you're trying to build up endurance through aerobics, swimming, or running, here's a way to check out progress and ensure safety while you work out. This Portable Heart Window can track your pulse rate during strenuous exercise, or measure your heart's recovery rate immediately after working out. By pressing a sensor button, the unit's microchip technology provides an accurate read-out on the LCD display. It comes built into a digital watch with a twenty-four-hour alarm. An excellent tool for those serious about exercise. **(I)**

BIOFEEDBACK MACHINE

There's a lot of talk today about stress management. All across the country people are attending seminars, taking oriental marshal arts courses, and meditating. Biofeedback is one method that has become increasingly popular. With this palm sized unit, you can relax yourself safely by applying the principles of biofeedback to state-of-the-art technology. First, place your fingers against the unit's sensing plates. You'll hear a tone. As your tension increases or decreases the tone changes its pitch. The machine can judge minute changes in the size of your skin pores—an instant and accurate measure of stress levels. There's a cassette tape to help you relax, but your concentration is the key. The tone can help you determine when you're likely to experience high-stress levels. **(I)**

AUTOMATIC DIGITRONIC

Do you or a loved one have high blood pressure? It's an ailment that affects millions of Americans. A sudden sharp rise or drop in blood pressure may be a warning sign of a heart attack. If you need frequent checks for this problem, Digitronic is a monitor worth considering. This easy to use blood pressure machine is an accurate method of keeping track of your status in-between doctor visits. The Digitronic inflates and deflates a measuring cuff automatically to a selected level. A large LCD display screen digitally shows you your pulse and pressure. With the touch of a button, the machine's built-in printer types out your systolic/diastolic pressures, the pulse rate, date, and time of reading. It's conveniently small for the elderly and weighs only two pounds. **(M)**

THE FREESTANDING WET/DRY SAUNA

Anyone conscious of fitness and good health knows that taking a sauna or steam is one of the best things to do for your body. Not only does it relax muscles and help skin breathe, sitting in a sauna can also be a soothing, effective way to dissolve stress. Now you don't have to join an expensive health club just to take advantage of the sauna facilities. The Freestanding Wet/Dry Sauna can be built right outside your home, near the pool, or it can be installed indoors. This 6' x 6' x 6' (182.88 cm) sauna is hand-finished and made of finger-jointed Western Red Cedar. For comfortable seating, it comes with two 14" x 62" (35.56 x 157.48 cm) benches that seat up to six people. Specially selected igneous gabbro rocks that will not crack or powder under extreme temperature changes are also a feature. The sauna heats up to 165° (74°C) in only twenty minutes. All electrical components of the 6000-watt stainless-steel heater are sealed to eliminate any contact with water and electric temperature and time controls are built in. The sauna comes with an interior faucet that can be attached to a garden hose or permanently plumbed to provide water for steam; a pre-installed floor drain can be connected to an existing interior drain or to a drip pan. A 29" x 43" (73.66 x 109.22 cm) door has a tinted Plexiglass window and all the hardware is brass-plated steel. The sauna takes about four hours to assemble with simple hand tools and weighs 700 lbs. (317 kg). **(E)**

SCULLERS ERGOMETER

This machine may look outdated but it's actually a very sophisticated piece of equipment. The only exercise rowing machine to simulate actual rowing conditions, the Sculler Ergometer will make you feel just like you're pulling through the water. The chrome-plated heavy-gauge steel and hardwood frame supports a precision-geared direct-drive chain mechanism and an open-spoked flywheel with plastic wind blades. The rotation of the flywheel creates an air resistance that recreates the actual water drag on the hull of a boat. As the flywheel builds momentum with each stroke, the rower feels a sense of acceleration just as if he or she were building speed in the water. The resistance level can be easily controlled by engaging different drive-chain sprockets and a speedometer and odometer tell you exactly how much energy you're expending. The foot pedals are fully rotating and feet are held firmly in place by adjustable nylon straps. A contoured seat glides smoothly on the chrome-plated frame and features sealed ball-bearing rollers that never need lubricating. **(M)**

HEALTH CLUB ROWING MACHINE

Rowing is possibly one of the best exercises for a total body workout. A rowing machine provides both aerobic and anaerobic exercises and increases respiratory and cardiovascular fitness as it develops and tones all major muscle groups. There's no better way to insure this total fitness than the Health Club Rowing Machine. Acknowledged by experts as the best machine on the market, this model has been used for training by the U.S. World Cup Ski Team. The Health Club Rowing Machine has a range of resistance adjustments from 10 to 300 pounds (about 4 to 112 kg) and the oars go through their full range of motion at any resistance setting, unlike other models whose oar movement is restricted as resistance is increased. Cushion-gripped stainless-steel oars are bolted directly to the frame and have moving parts which need no lubrication. The padded vinyl seat glides on a unique ball-bearing system for smooth, easy movement and foot pads pivot for maximum leg control and comfort. Adjustable Velcro bonds secure feet. This machine stores easily, measures 52" x 30" x 9" (132 x 76 x 23 cm^3) and weighs only 30 lbs. (11.19 kg). Get a better body and increase your aerobic capacity in the privacy of your own home with this professional piece of equipment. You'll feel better for it and you'll look better, too! **(M)**

The Bathroom

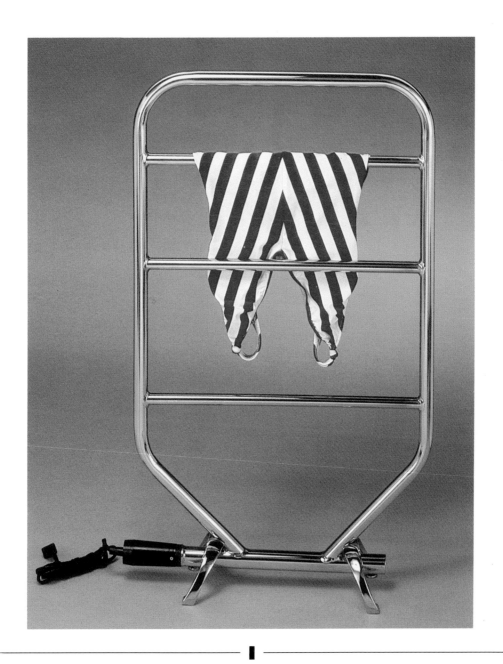

THE ENGLISH HEATED TOWEL STAND

Jackie O spent $10,000 to heat her towels. You can get that same luxury for much less. By circulating oil heated to 180°F (82.2°C) through an enclosed element, the seamless, brass-plated steel rails keep your towels warm and dry. The heat is sufficient to even dry bathing suits. It's self contained, works from household outlets, and requires no plumbing. The Towel Stand can even take the chill out of your bathroom. Hot but not harmful to touch, it dries robes, shirts, lingerie, and dish towels. Both floor and wall models come in chrome or brass. **(M)**

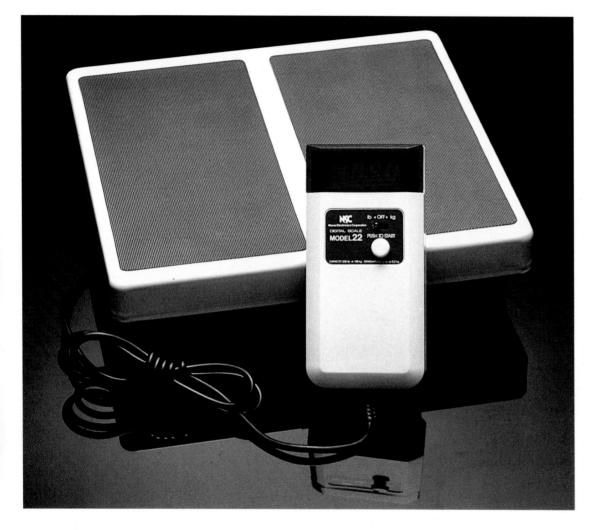

NOVUS DIGITAL BATHROOM SCALE

Fed up with bending down to manually adjust the scale every morning? If you're tired of that incorrect, frozen dial, or just sick of squinting to read the numbers, this digital device can take the guesswork out of weight measurement. Its easy-to-see LCD readout can be hand held or wall-mounted. The scale measures by the ½ lb or ¼ k, up to 300 lbs (136 kg). Once you step off, it automatically resets to zero. Don't be at a "loss" for words when you step down from the doctor's scale. This device can keep unknown weight off. **(I)**

ONLY TALKING SCALE WITH MEMORY

It could be the ultimate in satisfaction, or the height of embarrasment. This microprocessor-controlled scale automatically announces your weight in pounds or kilograms in a clear, digitally synthesized voice. If you're masochistic or want an ego boost, the scale will tell you how much you've gained or lost since your last weighing. After saying "goodbye," or, if you prefer, "have a nice day," the machine shuts itself off. There are five separate memory buttons for your entire family and even a guest button without memory. The machine announces "my battery is low" and even "overload," if someone's over 287 lbs (130.3 Kg). Volume controlled, batteries included. **(M)**

THE GROOMSMAN II

Ever wonder why you can't duplicate your barber's perfect beard trim? Frustrated that your sideburns and mustache seem to look great only after a haircut? A steady hand helps, but those expensive electric barber shears make all the difference. Now you can have that same well-groomed professional look every day. Most electric shavers have some trimming feature, but they are generally unwieldy and often cut a little more than you had anticipated. Don't walk around with uneven sideburns. This simple gadget is more effective than scissors or a razor. Its precision-ground blades neatly trim the toughest beards, sideburns, mustaches, or necklines. It's compact for traveling. Move around looking your best without missing that foreign barber's technique. **(I)**

HANDS-FREE SHOWER PHONE II

The shower scene from "Psycho" never could have taken place if this device had been around back then. Receive and make calls as you shower with this state-of-the-art device. You never have to miss a call again. In a hurry? Conduct your personal and professional business to save time by calling others. Feeling threatened? There are two special emergency buttons carried in memory. You can quickly call for help to cut off an unexpected intruder. For normal use, a flashing light ringer alerts you to incoming calls. Touch a button and answer through the built in speaker. There's also a volume control. An on/off switch hangs up when you're finished. Safe even when wet. **(I)**

HEATED TOILET SEAT

You've just spent that cold night snug under the covers. Waking up but still half asleep, you sit down on that freezing toilet seat. Whoa! That cold, hard seat would send shivers up anyone's spine. With this heated toilet seat your trips to the bathroom will be much more comfortable. Adjustable heat controls range from 84° to 102° F (28.8° to 38.8°C). You choose the comfort. This plastic seat is standard size and replaces any regular toilet seat. No tools are required. **(M)**

WET DUET PULSATING SHOWER MASSAGE

A luxury spa right in your own home. This dual shower device provides twin pulsating shower heads to stimulate and massage your body. Tired and aching muscles from a hard day's work? Relax them fast. The device fits shower enclosures from 55'' to 65'' (140 cm to 165 cm). It easily replaces your current shower head. Set up your own private spa. **(I)**

INFRALUX

Oh that aching muscle! You've taken a bath, you've gotten a massage, but it still hurts. This therapeutic heat source can provide relief. Using infrared heat, Infralux soothes muscle tension. It can also help with backache, arthritis, bursitis, and tennis elbow. The infrared heat stimulates a fresh supply of blood to the affected area, to quickly help relieve your aches and pains. It plugs into any wall outlet and has an adjustable heat setting for personal comfort. **(I)**

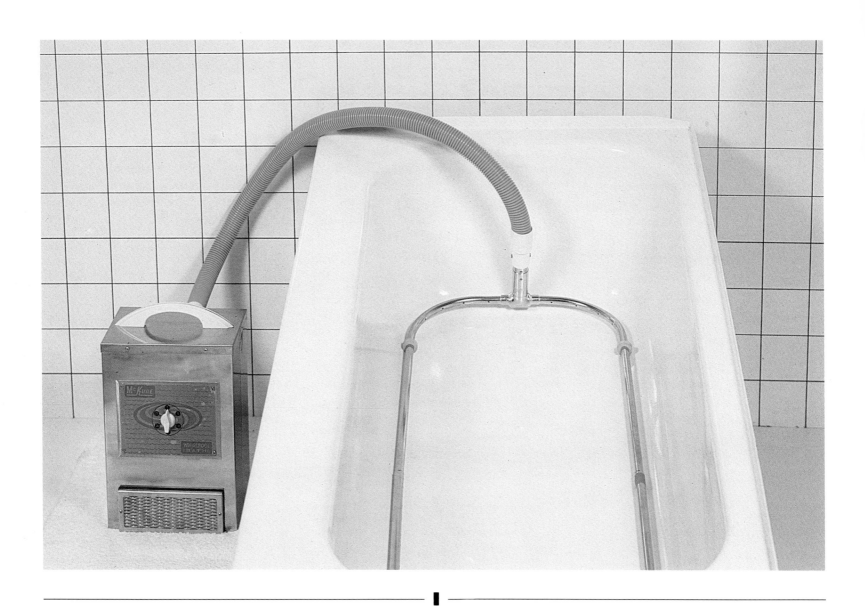

WHIRLPOOL BATHTUB CONVERTER

Another great relaxation tool. If you live in the city, or don't want to spend the dough on a Jacuzzi or hot tub, this whirlpool converter is the next best thing. It turns your boring tub into a relaxing spa in seconds. Great for relief of pain and discomfort caused by muscle exertion, circulatory ailments, or nervous tension. A 1-HP motor sits outside the tub and circulates two hundred gallons (757 l) of water per minute with adjustable intensity. Air is forced through a 60″ (152 cm) flexible plastic connecting hose to the perforated tube placed at the base of the tub. Jets of air and water rush around. Joints, ligaments, and muscles are relieved while circulation increases. There are no wires and no electricity near the water. A built-in thirty-minute timer lets you sit back and relax. There's no installation. It's not as glamorous as your own hot tub, but it does do the job. There's no better way to relax. (E)

ROTARY NOSE HAIR CLIPPER

Tired of seeing a jungle every time you look inside your nose? This precision electronic instrument can blaze that trail of unwanted hair down to size. If you frequently get colds, or congested sinuses, then you know how uncomfortable nostril hair can be when dried up mucous is present. With this professionally designed device, you will trim those unattractive follicles without a fuss. Why take the chance of sticking yourself with scissors? The unit's surgical steel exterior contains a safe rotating cutting edge. The edge is protected by a tubular guard that removes hair in just a single motion without pulling or jabbing. It's great for cutting a path to those hard-to-reach places. **(C)**

ILLUMINATED MULTI-ANGLE EXTENSION MIRROR

Sometimes, the hardest part of putting on makeup or shaving is seeing what you're doing. This illuminated magnifying extension mirror makes pampering yourself pleasant. No need to strain an eye just to apply mascara. The mirror folds flat against the wall and swings out 15″ (38 cm) to give you a clear view from any angle. There's a ring of shadow-free light to facilitate shaving. It also makes putting on makeup a breeze. The adjustable tension swivel lets you tilt and turn the 7¼″ (18.4 cm) diameter glass mirror in any direction. Need to share the sink with your partner? No problem. Finally you won't have to fight over the light or the medicine chest mirror. The 35-watt, ten-thousand-hour fluorescent bulb also eliminates fogging. It comes with screws and takes only minutes for easy wall mounting. The mirror provides three times the magnification than normal and uses regular current. **(I)**

THE SHOWER RADIO

S*inging in the rain?* Hardly. Many people love to sing along in the shower, but studies show most radio listeners shift channels quite frequently these days. Few, however, will step outside the shower to switch stations, even when the next tune up doesn't go with the flow. Well, here's a completely waterproof radio that lets you control your shower's musical environment while you get clean. The shower radio mounts on to any bathroom wall with a 2'' (5 cm) Velcro strip. Its 3'' (7.6 cm) speaker is loud enough to be heard over the splash and spray of your shower. Battery operated, it's portable for regular use as well. Go ahead, sing till your heart's content. **(I)**

THE HOME WATER STILL

N*ewspapers report* daily stories of polluted wells and poisoned municipal water systems. Bacteria, chemicals, rust, and other unpleasant tasting effluents are ruining our most valuable resource. Consequently, more and more people are purchasing expensive bottled water for home drinking use. If you've missed the taste of a cool, clean glass of water, The Home Water Still can bring back that refreshing feeling. The unit produces up to four pure gallons each day, for cooking, drinking, mixing beverages, or making ice cubes. A patented aluminum 720-watt heating mechanism safely boils tap water, creating steam and destroying any germs. The water vapor condenses on another anodized, patented, aluminum interior and becomes liquid, leaving chemical, mineral, and bacteriological impurities behind. Distilled water lets your foods and beverages taste more natural. It also helps keep appliances that use water free from mineral deposits. The Distiller has FDA and EPA approval and requires no plumbing or installation. Plugs into any household outlet. **(M)**

GYROSCOPIC RAZOR

Tired of arguing every morning over who uses the one bathroom outlet? Sick of renting adapters just so you can shave while traveling abroad? With this unique razor, you won't have to cut into that money clip ever again. There're no batteries and no electricity. Just pull on the cord and the gyroscopic action activates the blades. Self-sharpening, they spin at 45,000 cuts per minute, four times faster than electric shavers. Get clean shaven without any trouble or cost. **(I)**

ELECTRONIC THERMOMETER

The glass thermometer may be the most dangerous home-use medical device. With little children, there's always the chance of it breaking, either in their mouths or rectally. This poses many health hazards, including mercury poisoning. The glass is also extremely difficult to read. More often than not you will misjudge the numbers. This Electronic Thermometer gives hospital-accurate readings in just sixty seconds. It displays the exact temperature with an easy-to-read LCD display. If you forget to shut it off, the device stops automatically after eight minutes. There's an indicator that tells if you're low on batteries and also a calibration indicator. Batteries are included for a life of over three hundred hours. **(C)**

The Workroom

EQUAL-ARM BORING HOLE

Ever try to cut a circle in the middle of a wooden board? It's tough. Many people find it overwhelmingly difficult to replace or build woodwork. Here's a simple device to calm some of these concerns. Rather than struggle with a jigsaw, this boring tool lets you cut exact circles or perfect holes to accommodate your needs. It can be used in a drill press or a bit brace, on wood, plastic (except fiberglass), and thin metals. It cuts either inside or outside the diameter holes up to 4¾" (12.06 cm) diameter, to a depth of ⅞" (approx. 2.29 cm). If you cut from both sides, it cuts to 1¾" (4.44 cm) depth. Two center pieces are provided—a standard style, twist drill, and a brad-point tip for thin materials. For convenience the boring arm is indexed in both metric and SAE scales. **(I)**

STUD SENSOR

Sick of hammering in nails just to find the wall studs? Have you ever had to replaster or repaint a wall just to put up a few shelves? Welcome to do-it-yourself America. This device will save you the time and trouble of fixing a surface or looking up construction dimensions whenever you have to attach something to your walls. It lets you see electronically through walls to locate the studs. Reportedly, standard magnetic stud sensors don't really find the beams. They only "see" the metal nails. This doesn't reveal how wide the stud really is. However, this special Stud Sensor finds the actual supports by electronically measuring their change in density. It will tell you not only a stud's exact dimensions, but also will reveal its actual center. An LED light signals a change in mass as the unit passes over the edge of a stud or joist. Once past, the Stud Sensor tells you its actual width. For shelving, hanging pictures, or installing new wiring, this device can save your wall surface. It works on Sheetrock, plaster, wood, or acoustic ceiling and uses a 9-volt battery. Don't bang your head against that wall any longer. Size up that stud. **(I)**

SONIC EAR VALVES

If you live in a noisy city or work around heavy machinery, you know the dangers of loud sounds. Trains whizzing by, the constant thud of a pile driver—all of this can create more than eighty-five decibel levels, which can seriously damage your hearing. Many people use cotton or plastic as ear plugs. Unfortunately, these cut out all sounds so you can't tell what's going on. They also eliminate needed air circulation, unbalance air pressure, and create a clogged feeling. Well, these airflow, noise-dampening ear valves block out annoying noises, but discriminate with conversation and other normal sounds. A highly sophisticated inner ear reduces noise to pleasant levels. Conversation and other regular sounds are barely affected. The pliable silicone fits comfortably in your ears. Don't tune out life just to protect your hearing. **(C)**

SUPERSENSITIVE WATER ALARM

If you live in low-lying flood areas, this inexpensive device can be a real property saver. Just place it on your basement floor. The alarm goes off when there's as little as ⅛" (.317 cm) of standing water. Don't sleep after a big rainstorm? You'll be able to save that television and other expensive high-tech items that might be in the downstairs den. It's also great for boats if you're concerned about potential leaks in the hull. The unit operates on a 9-volt battery that's not included. Don't let a leak or flood dry out your bank account. **(I)**

PRECISION OILER

The high-tech revolution hasn't digitalized everything yet. Many mechanical items like clocks, instruments, and business machines still require periodic maintenance. Use this Precision Oiler to put oil exactly where it's needed. There's no longer a need to create a big mess when you're working on finely tuned parts. Hand pressure, not gravity, controls the flow—letting you oil hard to reach places. It can use any viscosity, from light or watch oil to heavy motor. There's another feature. When you release the pressure, excess oil is sucked back automatically into the transparent reservoir, giving you exact control to the tiniest fraction of a drop. No more slippin' and slidin'. **(C)**

AERATOR SANDALS

Take care of your lawn while you walk. Walking on growing grass doesn't help, but these Aerator Sandals can even speed things along. The twenty-six heavy spikes punch down the soil so that water and fertilizer can do their job better. Just strap them over your own footwear and walk the grounds. **(I)**

CALCUTAPE

If you do a lot of work around the house, or are involved in any engineering or construction activities this power tape measure could lend a hand. Calcutape converts inches and feet into metric measurements and vice versa. It converts length, volume, temperature, and weight. It also computes the circumference of a circle from its diameter. The device is also a calculator, featuring constant, square and power, reciprocal, and memory functions. Need precise measurements for roofing work? This unit provides Pythagorean calculations. The hypotenuse of a right triangle is most important for precise angles if you're a carpenter or contractor. Batteries included. **(I)**

CORNER SLIP SYSTEM

If you are building shelves and other storage units but don't want to spend much money, this Corner Clip System is a savings. The various plastic connectors let you build a desk, night stand, wall units, stereo cabinets, and countless other storage type amenities. Y connectors allow three pieces of wood to dove tail together. They're available in seven designer colors and have a modern, clean look. Excellent for college students and others just starting out. **(I)**

GLUE INJECTOR

If you love antiques, you'll love this item. Old furniture may look great, but it's guaranteed that the set of four chairs you just picked up from an auction will need regluing in two years. Sometimes, one small piece such as an arm needs tightening. Don't waste time disassembling or money on professional restorers. This needle-tip Glue Injector is over 1" (2.54 cm) long and tapers down to 1/16" (approx. 1mm) diameter. It can fit into hard-to-reach cracks and joints. It even flattens temporarily and goes around curves. A snap-on cap prevents the glue from drying or leaking. To refill, just pull out the plunger. The Injector also doubles as a fine point grease gun. It's made of polyethylene so it's completely unaffected by adhesives. **(C)**

FLEXLADDER

Tired of fruitlessly adjusting your ladder's angle to fix that tough job? Worried about support as you paint your house? Relax. This completely collapsible and adjustable ladder assumes as many shapes as you'll need. With rotating and flexible hinges, the Flexladder adjusts to any of three positions and then locks tight. In one angle, it lets two people work at once to finish a job in half the time. Need leverage for a tight spot? Now you can reach those stairway rungs. It has anti-slip metal rungs and stay-put rubber feet for safety. When you're finished with your chore the heavy duty aluminum metal collapses for easy storage. **(M)**

DOUBLE WEDGE ELECTRIC LOG SPLITTER

Don't waste much time swinging an axe just to play macho. There are more important things to do (such as playing with fun gadgets!). This device can save you hours by splitting an entire cord of wood in only ninety minutes. You'll get that warm feeling from firewood without the fuss. Its electric action uses a wedge at each end that allows you to split logs in both directions. After splitting a log, you don't wait for the ram to return to the starting position. This unit exerts up to ten tons of force and can handle logs up to 26" (66 cm) long and 18" (45.7 cm) in diameter. **(E)**

POWER-FLOW ROLLER PAINTING SYSTEM

Sick of manually painting rooms and exteriors? You don't want to pay professional painters but you don't trust the neighborhood teenager? Your dilemma may be over. No need to waste valuable time standing there with a brush. Power-flow can get the job done in minutes, and it looks like a professional's work. The unit sits right on top of your paint can. It pumps a continuous flow of paint through the custom designed 9" (22.9 cm) internal feedroller. Buttons on both sides control the paint flow through 20' (610 cm) of flexible hose. No need to drag that drippy can around the room. It's a mess-free way to paint. A 16" (40.6 cm) extension handle attaches to the hosing to reach ceilings and high spots. The pump starts working when you plug it in. It shuts off automatically at maximum working pressure between 25-40 psi. For cleaning, there's a quick-clean adapter that attaches to your garden hose or laundry tub faucet. It's easy. Forget paint spills or turpentine for those sticky, hard brushes. Just a quick paint job at an affordable price. **(I)**

LOG PRESS

Conservation of our natural resources has become a major focus in America today. Unfortunately, recycling paper to preserve forest timber is one area that isn't economically efficient. If the thought of throwing out piles of newspapers still bothers you, this device may help ease your social conscience. It doesn't recycle the paper but it does make use of its energy. The Log Press converts unwanted newspaper into slow-burning, energy-efficient fuel for your stove or fireplace. The device makes up to twenty-five energy-saving logs in just twenty-five minutes from a week's supply of old papers. The logs will burn for as much as an hour and a half, generating 7,500 BTUs per pound. According to the distributor, since the paper logs burn practically smoke and ash free their ash content is only 2.1 percent. Just soak your newspapers over-night in plain water. Then use the Press to convert pulp into easily stacked briquettes. It's simple to use and you can add sawdust or leaves to the pulp if desired. Just let them dry for three to ten days before starting up that fireplace or wood stove. You can use the briquettes alone, or to enhance normal log burning. The Log Press will help save on heating bills and should pay for itself within two weeks. **(I)**

HIGH REACH CHAIN SAW

Many homes are surrounded by trees that frequently grow too close for comfort. If you need to cut those yard trees down to size but are afraid to fight off that falling branch, let this safety chain saw do the dirty deed. Don't climb up a dangerous ladder holding an easily mishandled saw. This device can cut branches up to 30' (9.14 m) away while you stay put on the ground. The 24" (61 cm) cutting chain has eleven hardened teeth faced in opposite directions, so it cuts on each pull. Just throw the bag containing two 25' (7.62 m) ropes over any branch you want to cut, and alternatively pull the ropes. The instructions also demonstrate how to undercut branches to avoid tearing bark and harming the tree. **(I)**

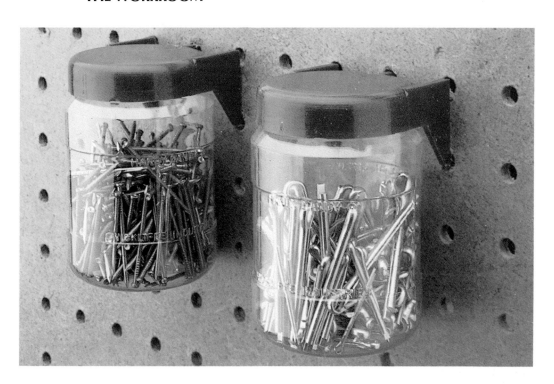

HANDI-HOOK

This multi-use tool will help eliminate your working hang-ups. It attaches in a snap to support whatever you need. Paint or watercans, buckets for cleaning, tools, and other equipment are at your fingertips while working on a ladder or scaffold. Outdoors or indoors, this simple device won't get you hung up reaching for something. (I)

PERFBOARD CONTAINERS

The most common problem in doing fix-it work is keeping track of nails and screws. Varying sizes and shapes confuse everyone when they're lumped together. Well, now you can get rid of those rusty cans and dirty containers and bring some organization to your life. Rather than spend hours hunting for a screw, these special containers will neatly satisfy your needs. Their tops attach to any Perfboard. Just unscrew the bottoms. (C)

INSTA-PUMP

Does your basement look like a swamp? No need to call the plumber to clean out that clogged sink. Here's a pocket-sized pump that can help you out of trouble. The Insta-Pump can pump over 50 gallons (189.2 l) in twenty minutes. But amazingly, it weighs only 8 oz (227 g). Using rechargeable NiCad batteries, this device is perfect for bailing you out of a boat jam. Taking on water fast? Insta-Pump is completely submersible and has a high impact case that's acid resistant. It will let you solve flooding and water removal problems without using expensive equipment. Other AC and DC current models are available that are even more powerful. Ask when you order. (I)

The Greenhouse

NELLORS GARDEN SEEDFEEDER

Now you can enjoy the fruits of a garden without the start-up time that turns some people off. Everyone loves fresh homegrown vegetables, but many of us can't spend the time necessary in the backyard. Well, this device opens soil, plants seeds, closes and marks rows, and deposits fertilizer all in one pass. There's no bending or stooping. Six interchangeable seed plates provide up to thirty-one different seed varieties, giving you a range of garden delights. The feeder plants them at intervals of 3" (7.6 cm), 3½" (8.9 cm), 4" (10.2 cm), or 9" (22.9 cm). It also holds up to 10 lbs (4.54 kg) of fertilizer that can be deposited at varying levels. A furrowing shoe turns and closes the soil automatically while adjusting for different planting depths. This complete feeder assembles easily with just hand tools. **(I)**

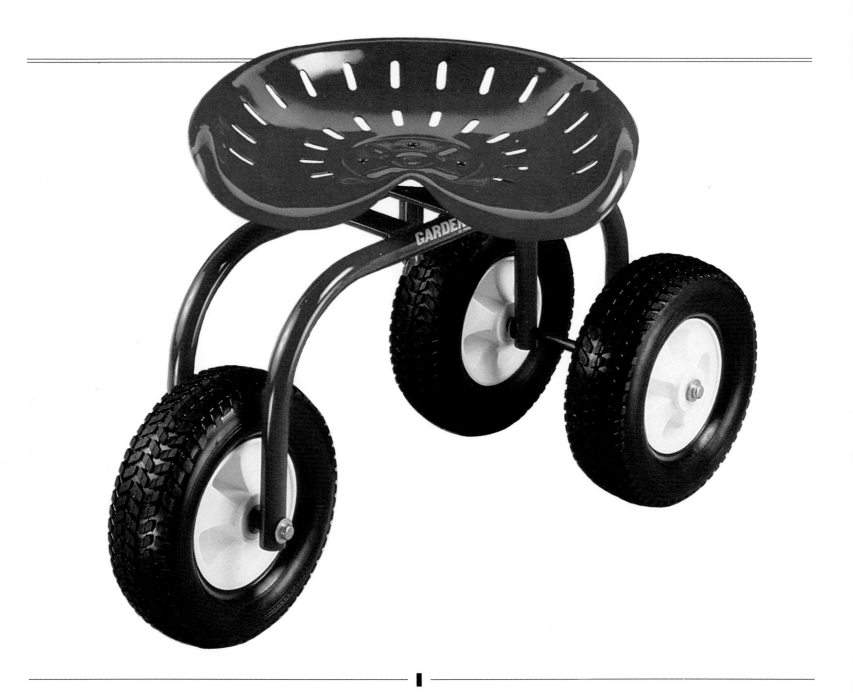

THE WORLD'S ONLY ROLLING GARDENER'S SEAT

If you like to spend time in your garden but have a bad back or other injury that prevents stooping, this device can weed out your difficulties. A simple tricycle-like moving seat lets you maneuver comfortably along garden furrows. A 360 degree swivel seat permits you to work facing any direction. Puncture-proof tires are wide enough to avoid getting bogged down in wet soil, while still allowing movement in cultivated dirt. Steel tubing supports up to 400 lbs (181.44 kg). The seat is also good for painting, yard work, and other ground related chores. **(l)**

PH METER

Take some of the guesswork out of gardening. This unique meter lets you measure the acid/alkaline composition of your soil to help you grow healthier plants. Just insert the probe into your soil and within a minute you get an accurate reading. Is acid rain or chemical pollution hurting your immediate countryside? Nail those polluters quickly with some proof. There're no batteries to wear down. It comes with complete directions for the most popular grasses, fruits, vegetables, shrubs, trees, herbs, spices, and even houseplants. Offers you advice if your soil isn't in the right range. **(I)**

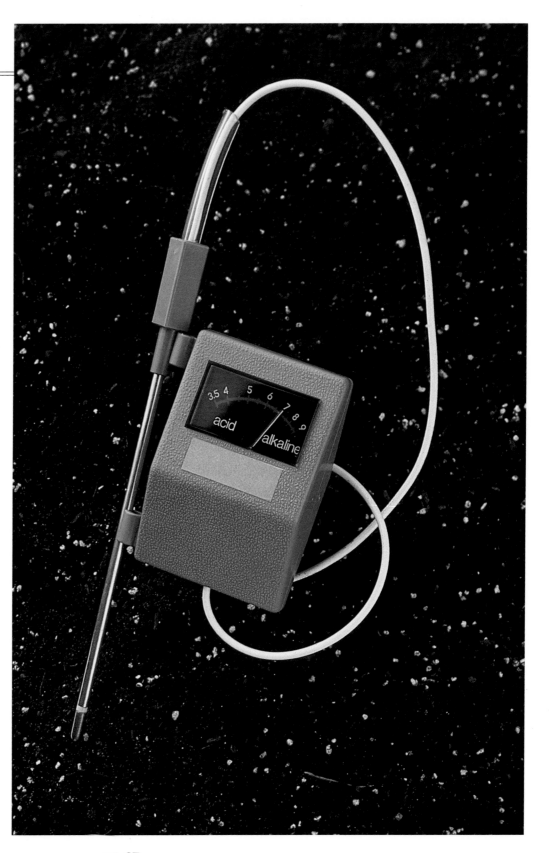

ULTRASONIC BIRD DISCOURAGER

You can forget that scarecrow forever. If you have crops or a nice garden, chances are that uninvited guests from the ground and from the air often come for dinner. Well, here's something that effectively protects your garden against unwanted guests. This simple device emits an ultrasonic hum that you probably won't hear but that sends birds off to roost elsewhere. It's a specially designed tape that vibrates in even the lightest breeze so that there's no need for electronic maintenance or wires. It comes in 100' (30.5 m) spools, so you can spread or cut pieces as they're needed. Reportedly, gardeners in England swear by it. **(C)**

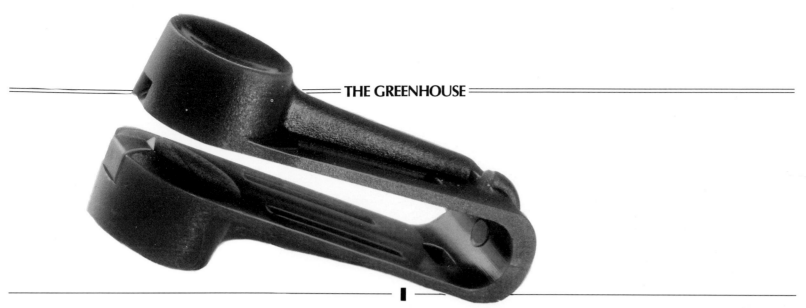

ZIP-IT-OPEN INSTANT BAG OPENER

Never struggle with opening a bag again. If you have delicate nails or tender skin, you know what havoc today's packaging can wreak. Sometimes, you can even cut your tongue or mouth trying to open certain types of containers. Not with this gadget. Zip-It-Open will miraculously release almost any type of sealed plastic, cellophane or polyethylene bag. Your teeth will never be at risk again. Just press down gently until the blade pierces that bag. Move the device right or left and zip...it's open. It fits in your pocket so you can use it anywhere. **(C)**

THREE AUTOMATIC WATERERS

How many times have you come back from a brief vacation only to find your lovely plants dying of thirst? Until we notice brown or drying leaves, many of us even forget to water plants that are right under our noses. No longer! This special device automatically feeds fluid to that fern. Most plants thrive on a constant rate of watering rather than usual feast or famine. To use these automatic waterers, just insert the tube's basket into the soil near the roots. Then take the weighted end and put it into a pot of water. When the reservoir's level is low, just refill. The device uses liquid fertilizer. **(C)**

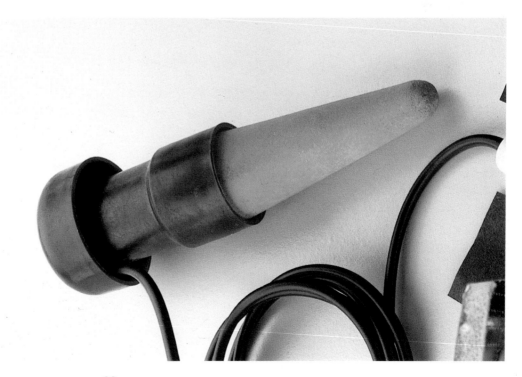

SOIL ANALYSIS GAUGE

Another helpful lawn and garden tool. Too much fertilizer can sometimes be a bad thing. But if your garden isn't growing, the soil may not be rich enough. How do you check? Try this automatic soil gauge. Within seconds it tells you whether you have enough or too much nitrogen and potash in your yard or garden. Just stick the probe into the earth and check the dial to see if you need fertilizer. There are no batteries to wear out. **(I)**

RAINMATIC

Set up an automatic sprinkler system for a fraction of the cost. Just attach the RainMatic device to any faucet and your simple garden hose becomes a sophisticatd sprinkler. A microprocessor will turn your hose on and off up to eight times a day from one to seven days a week. Day or night, even while you're away, RainMatic can be timed for one minute up to more than twelve hours. Need to keep that special strain of vegetation regularly soaked? It's as easy to program the RainMatic as it is to answer your phone. Set up a regular watering system, or switch to manual for individual jobs such as washing the car. Purchase four D cell alkaline batteries and start sprinkling. The unit locks onto faucets to prevent theft. **(I)**

CAN-DO DIGGER

Trying to dig a hole for that post or pole? Sick of having to work extra-hard just to get below the ground with a thin hole? With this Can-Do Digger, you only make a hole of the diameter you need—straight down. The patented posthole digger goes to a depth of 39" (99.1 cm) in hard soils. So you can fix that fence, put up a yard light, or reinforce a support. Try working with a shovel. You'll waste hours digging and then refilling. **(I)**

SAW/PRUNER

There's no longer a need to hire that expensive gardener. With this extra-long pruner, you can get shrubs and hard-to-reach tree limbs that even ladders can't angle. This solidly constructed tool is especially made for groundskeepers and gardeners, to keep them firmly on the ground. This pruner neatly slices up to one and one-eighth branches with the yank of a rope. The pulley system creates leverage so that it's easy to prune. Adjustable height goes up to 17' (5.185 m). There's also a 16" (40.6 cm) detachable saw for any hard-to-get branch. **(I)**

The Patio And The Porch

REFLECTING SUNTAN MAT

It gives a quick, natural tan, almost all year round. The Malor surface mat reflects the sun's rays so that you can tan on both sides simultaneously. Not hot to touch, it can keep your body warm and tan even when it's 50° F (10 C). You'll be tanned from spring through the fall. Only 4 lbs (1.82 kg), the thick foam padding can be used on concrete, sand, or anywhere. **(I)**

PET FOUNTAIN

Stop putting out water for "fido." Just connect this ingenious touch-operated valve to an outdoor hose, faucet, or Y-connector and you will always satisfy your pet's thirst. Your dog or cat will quickly learn that with an upward nudge or sideways pressure on the tip, they'll be rewarded with a gentle stream of cool water. It shuts off automatically so there's no mess. **(I)**

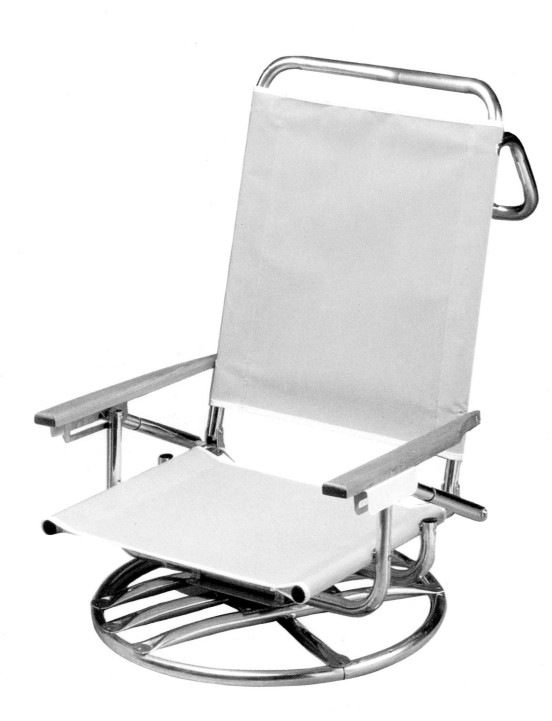

THE SUN-TRACKING FOUR POSITION BEACH CHAIR

Lazy in the backyard or at the beach? If you practice the ultimate in an easy lifestyle, laying in the sun is probably your favorite pastime. Well, now you can enhance your sun-worshiping by not even bothering to move an inch. This folding beach chair has a swivel base that rotates 360 degrees, allowing you to track along with the rays as the sun moves across the sky. You never need to move. Four adjustable position settings also let you go from completely upright to fully reclined. It's ideal for angling that perfect tan. The distributor says the aluminum construction is fifty percent thicker than most beach chairs and that the seats are made of a strong, commercial grade awning material. (I)

TELE-RANGER

If you have a portable telephone, then this gadget is a plus. Sometimes the convenience of portable phones is lost due to bad signals, interference, or limited range. If you want to sit out by your nearby lake, but are expecting an important phone call, there's no need to stay behind because your model won't make it. This device can extend the range of your portable phone up to 3 times, while improving its reception sensitivity. The Tele-Ranger antenna can take a standard 700' (213.355 m) model and stretch its range up to 2000' (609.6 m). If you have a newer 1000' (304.8 m) unit, you can go even farther without losing touch. It requires a simple plug installation. The adapter attaches to your phone base station. The antenna attaches to your roof. Thirty feet of connecting coaxial cable comes along with the unit, but you must supply the antenna mast. Specify make and model of your phone when ordering this long distance device. **(I)**

PATIO HOSE AND REEL

It's nothing new, but it is a real time-saver. We've all spent countless hours trying to unwind and rewind that stretched out garden hose. When you are in a hurry, there's nothing more annoying than struggling with loops that twist into strange directions. This Patio Hose and Reel attaches right on to your faucet so that it's always ready. No need to rummage around the garage. Just pull the head out and spray. When you're finished, the ⅝" diameter hose rewinds and collapses flat, like a professional fire hose. According to the distributor, it's completely safe to drink through the non-toxic liner. **(I)**

NEW LAVASTONE BARBECUE

The time for messy charcoal barbecuing may be over. Almost everyone loves the cooking flavor from an outdoor grill. But how many times has the thought of handling and cleaning up those messy coals prevented you from enjoying it? With the New LavaStone Barbecue, you can get the taste of charcoal cooking without the time and trouble. This system's magnesium-insulated heating unit readies natural LavaStone within five minutes. Charcoal takes much longer to get white hot. LavaStone Barbecue is run by a standard electric power source. Its thermostatic heat sensor signals you when it's just the right time to cook. Adjustable controls and a removable heat reflecting cover let you determine the barbecuing speed. When you're finished, just remove the stones for easy cleaning. They last indefinitely. **(M)**

SWIRLON ROTARY WASHER SCRUBBER

Faced with a tough cleaning job? There's no need to rely on "elbow grease" any longer when picking up dirt and grime. Start the easy high-tech life by taking advantage of this new rotary scrubber. Swirlon is a sudsing, rotating and rinsing, water powered appliance that will save you time and trouble. Just attach the device to your garden hose, and fill the built-in cup with detergent. The adjustable brush swivels to six different positions for reaching those hard-to-get places. Its pulsating rotation loosens dirt and filth within seconds. There's a built-in water control valve right on the handle, and aluminum extenders up to 70" (1.219 m) long for those out-of-reach spots. Swirlon's great for washing windows and cleaning patio furniture, garbage cans, and even the car. **(I)**

SQUIRREL RESISTANT BIRD FEEDER

If you love birds chirping in your backyard, but are tired of seeing squirrels eat up the seeds you've left, you'll love this bird feeder. Its 17" (43.2 cm) diameter hood has recessed feeding ports to keep squirrels out in the cold. But birds can perch and eat to their hearts' content. The clear acrylic construction protects feed from the wind and rain and lets you see who's coming to dinner. It holds 5 to 7 lbs (2.3 kg to 3.18 kg) of feed, so you won't need to refill frequently. The top lifts off easily for changing. There are four feeding perches and a 24" (61 cm) steel chain for hanging. Enjoy your feathered friends. **(I)**

AQUALUME MOONLIGHT

A moonlight swim can be a romantic's delight. If you are really into setting the perfect scene but don't want to spend a fortune to create the mood, then this device will turn you on. Don't even think about the expense of installing permanent pool-lighting fixtures. With Aqualume Moonlight, you can light up that above or in-ground pool, spa, or hot tub with subtle white light or lovely, glowing "mood colors." You and your friends will be dying to hop in for hours with this device. It's completely portable and there are no wires, but it's powerful enough to illuminate a 15'x 30' (4.57x 9.14 m) pool. Simple and safe to use, just push a button and drop the light into your pool. As it sinks to the bottom, you'll be swimming with delight. Operates on 8 D batteries or rechargeable nickel cadmium type. There's a rechargeable receptacle but you'll get thirty hours at a time of pool-time frolicking. **(I)**

SUNMIST

Another tanning helper for you sun worshipers. If you love the feel of a good tan but find the constant heat overwhelming, don't hide in the house. As you lay there, the Sun-Mist covers your entire body with a gentle spray of cool water. You'll be tanned and refreshed at the same time. Using the supplied fasteners, just attach Sun-Mist's clear plastic tubing to the outer rim of your own lawn chair. It attaches to a garden hose with a supplied connector. There's an on/off switch right there, so you can determine the intensity of the spray. Don't move an inch. Adjust your chair to any direction without disturbing SunMist. If you've got friends, one garden hose can hook up two or more units. **(I)**

FLOAT PHONE

Another great phone device. Not only can this model go into the shower—it floats,too. Relax out in the pool with the Webcor Float Phone. You'll never lose touch. It's completely waterproof so you can play around to your heart's content. The unit transmits up to 1000' (304.8 m) over the new FCC frequencies. Up to ten thousand possible digital codes keep other phones off your line. It's also pulse and tone switchable. The headset uses NI-CAD batteries which automatically recharge when the headset is returned to its base. The unit plugs into an AC outlet and a phone jack. Now there's no longer a need to wait around inside for important calls. Don't put off that poolside plunge. **(M)**

CHARCOAL STARTER

Another helpful quickie for the backyard barbecue. Getting coals started is a pain. Using lighter fluid can not only affect the taste of your food, but there is increasing evidence that it's not healthy. With this easy charcoal starter, you can start coals within five to ten minutes without lighter fluid. Just place the aluminized steel container on the grill. Crumple up some newspaper inside and add up to fifty briquettes. A wooden handle prevents you from burning your fingers when you pour out the coals. **(I)**

BIONIC EAR

Do you enjoy watching birds and animals in your backyard? Animals have interesting physical and communication behavior, but we miss out on much of their interaction because of our limited audio capacity. Our ears simply can't hear much of what goes on. If you are really into animal watching, now you can listen in as well. The Bionic Ear is a sensitive directional microphone that makes it possible to locate birds, game, or even unseen pests through sounds. If you're out in the woods, you can also help out rangers by finding lost children or hikers. This state-of-the-art device can pinpoint the foghorn on shore when you're out in a boat. You can also listen for intruders at your house or business location. Increase the directional sensitivity by purchasing an extra, hand held, parabolic dish. The Bionic Ear operates on a 9-volt battery that must be bought separately. Headphones have special individual volume controls to adjust for hearing differences. **(I)**

AUTOMATIC LIGHT SWITCH

If your needs are simple, there's no reason to spend money on expensive, computerized light switches. Just install this basic switch between a light bulb and the socket. When the sun goes down, the light comes on. It's great for outdoor flood lights, porch lamps, and even for inside your house while you're gone. Applicable for 110-volt sockets and rated for up to 150 watts. **(C)**

CITIZEN POCKET TV

This compact unit is designed to work best outside in sunlight. If you're sitting on the lawn but don't want to miss that ball game, this TV won't get "wiped out" by the sun. Most sets are difficult to watch when the sun's light rays hit. Just think how many times you've had to darken the room to see television indoors. With this 3"x 8" (7.6 x 20.3 cm) set, a special LCD panel allows light to pass through and create an amazingly sharp picture. The brighter the sun light, the better the picture. For indoor viewing, the electro-luminescence, back-lighting attachment fits over the screen panel to provide additional brightness when needed. There's also a built-in AM radio. Four power supplies are available for maximum mobility. It comes with batteries and an AC adapter. Optional features are an auto adaptor and a rechargeable battery pack. Specify when ordering. Now you can enjoy T.V. anywhere. **(M)**

MAIL ALERT

Expecting that important letter? No need to keep checking the mail box to see if the postman has arrived. If you live in the country or suburbs, constant dressing up just to run outside during a cold winter day is not very pleasant. With Mail Alert, you'll know if that package is present. When the mailman opens the box, a bright yellow steel plate flips up. You can come out to collect. A screwdriver connects the 4" x 5¼" (10.2 x 13.33 cm) flag. It meets all postal service regulations so you won't hassle with the government. **(C)**

DELUXE POOL ALARM SYSTEM

Having a swimming pool can be a great experience, but if there are little children playing around, you always have to worry that they might fall in. Don't live in fear about your own backyard. This Deluxe Pool Alarm System monitors your pool twenty-four hours a day. If a child or pet accidentally falls in, an alarm sounds both outside and inside your house—and can be heard 200' (609.6 m) away. The Pool Alarm has an adjustable sensitivity as it floats on the water surface. The household remote unit works on standard current. You just turn it off when taking a dip. Protect that hot tub, country pond, or pool. **(I)**

TAN-O-METER

If you love a dark tan but have a tendency to stay out in the sun too long, don't spend those first days of summer sulking in the shadows. With Tan-O-Meter, you'll know exactly how strong the sun is at any moment so you can plan your tanning time accordingly. This meter accurately measures the sun's ultra-violet rays. It's great for overcast periods when the sun can fool you with its intensity. There's a built-in timer/alarm to keep you from burning. **(I)**

The Garage And The Car

Gadgets

ADJUSTABLE LUMBAR MASSAGING SEATBACK

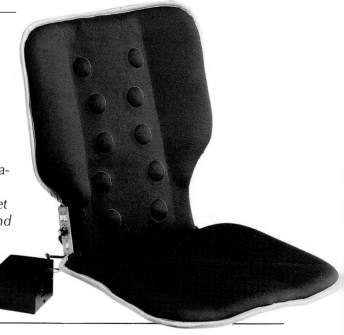

If you drive professionally, or just frequently sit behind the wheel, your back will thank you for this seat. Reportedly used by Japanese taxi drivers, this massaging seat cushion offers electronically controlled lumbar support that adjusts to your back for riding comfort. When the strain of driving in bad weather is intense, you know your back is the first place to feel it.

Built into this device, two vertical cables are connected to the flexible steel back frame, so you control the height and depth of the two cross bars. They adjust to your individual needs. A variable dial controls vibrations at any rate between 1700 RPM and 3800 RPM. Let the comfortable foam-padded frame and underseat put the ease back into your driving and take the tension away. **(M)**

KNIGHT HAWK II CAR ALARM

Most people with good automobiles spend top dollar after they've been burned by robbery or theft. But with this inexpensive, fully portable car alarm, you'll get the protection you need but without the price. The Hawk II detects entry, glass breaking, and other unwanted internal motions within your car, night or day. It plugs into your cigarette lighter. Just turn the key and it's armed. The unit gives you sixty seconds to lock up the car and fifteen seconds when you enter. If you're late, or if crooks come calling, the unit sends out a two minute blast at eight decibels. The flashing red light also warns of prowlers. If the thief discovers the unit's plug and pulls it out, batteries take over and continue the sounds. If the crook continues, the blast remains on. It's also helpful if you break down on the highway. The flashing red light lets motorists know you need help, a terrific safety feature. **(I)**

CARBON MONOXIDE DETECTOR

Carbon monoxide can be a killer. It's odorless, tasteless, and invisible. Even small leaks from your heating unit or in your car can cause recurring headaches and fatigue. With this special device, you can check out potential hazards and keep yourself and your loved ones safe. A red caution light comes on even if there's .01 percent concentration in the air. If the level increases to 0.4 percent (which is a life threatening situation after three hours), a buzzer and a flashing red danger light sound the alarm. The device is effective within a 400 sq ft (37 sq m) range, so you can keep your home, car, or plane free from fumes. There are separate models, specify when ordering. **(C)**

FLEXSTAND ROPE TOW

If you've ever broken down or gotten stuck in bad weather, then you know how important a good tow rope is. Remember the last time you needed help? More often than not the rope snapped or created such a shock when the slack was taken up that you could have sued for whiplash. No longer. This West German rope is rated for 5,500 lbs (2494.74 kg) and is only 5' (152 cm) long when not being used. But when you begin to pull, it stretches to 15' (457 cm). This lessens the slack and the shock. Spring-loaded catches on both hooks ensure added safety. Made of highly visible yellow polypropylene, it weighs only 1½ lbs (681 kg). **(I)**

CHARGE IT

You're late for work and the car's battery won't start. Sound familiar? It happens to thousands of people every day. Rather than suffer the loss of time and cost of a tow or an outside service call, you might consider

Charge It as a precautionary tool. If you're frequently running to meet deadlines or live in difficult weather climates, this portable power source can take the paranoia out of rushing. Just plug the unit into your cigarette lighter

and within five to ten minutes the battery will be completely recharged. If you're an adamant non-smoker, a battery clip is available. There's also a conversion adapter to power most 12-volt appliances. **(M)**

REMOTE CAR STARTER

It's below freezing outside and you've got to get to work tommorrow. If you're concerned that the battery won't make it overnight, you'll probably start her up before getting into bed just to improve your chances. Well, don't stumble around the garage at midnight. This device lets you start the car from the comfort of your bed. Some people just hate to get into a freezing machine in the morning. This device lets you heat up or cool off the car's interior as needed without stepping outside. Winter or summer, just pre-set your heat or air-conditioning controls. There's no problem with theft because the steering wheel stays locked. **(E)**

SPOTLIGHT INFLATOR

Another brilliant car device. If your tire has a small leak, there's no need to get panicky out there on the highway. This combination emergency light and air compressor will reinflate your tire and get you going to the nearest gas station. The powerful 135 lb PSI compressor works from your cigarette lighter to inflate that car or motorcycle tire fast. The beam of light lets you see what you're doing. Inside the unit is a 2' (61 cm) inflator house and an 8' (203.2 cm) connecting cord. An easy-to-read pressure gauge is built-in. The light comes with a removable red emergency lens to warn passing motorists. **(I)**

INSTANT SPARE TIRE INFLATOR

You're rushing off to an appointment for a big job. Or perhaps your loved one needs to get to the hospital immediately. As you try and zip away, you discover a disabling flat tire. There is just no time to change it. Sound familiar? With Instant Spare Tire, you're on your way in minutes. The special synthetic rubber compound inflates and seals quickly, so you're off promptly. Just shake the can, attach the flexible nozzle to the tire valve and press the button. The 15 oz (425.2 g) can completely inflate one tire, or partially inflate several. **(C)**

RADAR DETECTOR MIRROR

If you spend your life playing cat and mouse with "smoky" on the road, then this sophisticated device is perfect for your car. Radar detectors are illegal in many states. The police sometimes look all around the dash to see if you're cheating when they notice a sudden drop in speed. With this microprocessor-controlled unit, your car will be fully equipped, but the police won't know it. The Radar Detector Mirror mounts right over your own rear view mirror. If they pay a call, the cops won't suspect. Just hang something and it will look like ornamentation. There are no screws or tools. The sequence of red lamps lights up as a radar signal comes closer. If you're in the immediate signal area, the lights blink in sequence. Unlike most standard models, this device picks up radar from both the front and the rear of your car. There's a removable plug with a power cord so that you can play it cool if necessary. **(M)**

SAV-A-LIFE

You and your family are out for a lovely drive through the country. The rolling hills pass by silently, lulling you into a serene state. Suddenly, a deer rushes out from the trees running across the road. You swerve to try and avoid it, but the car goes into a skid quite possibly crashing. It happens to thousands of people each year as both large and small animals dart across our highways. This device can provide security for both your car and the animals that may unknowingly cross its path. Sav-a-Life is an ultrasonic warning system that will warn wild animals to stay away from that road while you pass. It attaches easily to a front bumper or car grill. When traveling over thirty mph, the device creates an ultrasonic warning siren. It's inaudible to you, but deer, skunks, raccoons, and chipmunks will freeze in their tracks before running on to the road. Comprised of two units, it's smaller than a cigarette lighter. You never know, the life you save may be your own. **(I)**

MAP METER

You're driving in unfamiliar territory and your car is almost out of gas. The nearest station is miles away. From the map, there are many choices, but you need the shortest road. Can't measure because of curved lines? Relax. The Opisometer will tell you the shortest way, no matter how windy the road. Just trace the route over the map with its wheel. There's no complicated arithmetic. The counter displays map distance in inches. You get mileage using the map's scale. It resets easily to zero if you're checking alternatives in a hurry. Need to get somewhere quick but confused over directions? This precision Opisometer gets you there faster. **(C)**

HEADLIGHT REMINDER

It's simple but sweet. The most common problem we all have with our cars is a dead battery. How many times have you gone off for an evening—had a lovely time—but came back to a car that won't start? Standing miles from nowhere at two in the morning, your pleasant outing becomes a nightmare. Usually, someone forgot to shut off the headlights. No longer. This device sounds a buzzer if the lights are still on after the ignition is off. Just connect the alligator clips or adapter bars to your car's fusebox. An adhesive strip mounts the device instantly. The distributor swears that this device can not damage the car's electrical system. An in-line diode prevents incorrect hookup. It fits or can be adapted to most cars. **(C)**

CAR FINDER

It's two o'clock in the morning and you've just walked off an airplane after a week's business trip. As you stagger exhaustedly into the parking lot, you realize you've forgotten where you parked the car. Sound familiar? Don't spend hours hunting through that maze of metal. The Car Finder will get you on your way in minutes. Just touch this device and your car will honk its horn and flash its lights. You'll spot it in seconds. The device is a miniature transmitter that attaches itself to any key chain. It's effective from up to 750' (229 m) away. If you're walking to your car and it seems as though someone's following you, just press Car Finder and it appears as though there's a person waiting in the car, a good security device. **(I)**

FIREBAN

The fear of fire after a car crash is frightening to everyone. We've all seen television shows and movies where loved ones are lost to fire. While the frequency may not be as great as we imagined, there's no harm in playing it safe. Fireban helps prevent car fires by automatically shutting off your auto's electrical supply. And it does it within six milliseconds of a collision. This is most important because in crashes of twenty-two mph or more, most vehicle fires are caused by electrical short circuits. The device also helps guard your car against theft. Just turn the key and the entire ignition and electrical system is cut off. Only you can restart it. **(I)**

LIGHT-UP READER

Finding your way while driving at night can be a hazardous undertaking. Trying to read a map by the dashboard light while keeping one eye on the road is a good way to cause an accident. This light-up map is a safety precaution no glove compartment should be without. Easily plugged into the car cigarette lighter, this device illuminates maps and directions. A special spot magnifier zeroes in on the fine print and insets. Made with tough, transparent plastic, 8″ x 5⅛″ (20.32 x 12.7 cm) this Light-up Reader comes with its own vinyl pouch that keeps it free from dust. **(C)**

DRIVE ALERT

We've all experienced the life threatening experience of almost falling asleep at the wheel. The constant flashing of light and monotonous drone of a car engine can lull almost anyone into a state of drowsiness—each year, thousands of motorists lose their lives because of it. Well, here's a simple device that literally could save your life while you drive. It attaches behind your ear. Should you happen to nod off on the road, the unit will wake you up quickly with a sharp electronic beep. Salespeople, truck drivers, or cross-country vacationers can benefit from this comfortable device. You can't even feel it until it counts. **(I)**

EASY LIFT MODEL 1

You're out on the highway at night. Suddenly you blow a tire. It's freezing cold and just the thought of having to jack-up the car manually sends shivers up your spine. With Easy Lift·automobile jack, you'll never have to worry again. This ingenious device actually uses your own car's exhaust for lift. It creates a cushion of air, so changing that tire becomes a breeze. It can be used anywhere—on sand, mud, or snow—even on uneven surfaces and slopes, where a normal jack is impossible to use. Put the Easy Lift hose over the exhaust tail pipe. Start up your motor and within fourteen seconds your car will rise to a height of 20″ (51 cm). Two additional models work with larger cars, boats, and trailers. Specify the size when ordering. **(I)**

Security Gadgets

BEEP-N-KEEP KEY FINDER

This is the ultimate time and anxiety reliever. Some people spend up to half an hour each day hunting for their house keys. As they run around blindly, they're frantically thinking about being robbed or worse. No longer. If it's business as usual trying to get out the door under a deadline, don't even think twice. Just snap your fingers or clap your hands four times. This ingenious device attaches to your key chain and will "answer" with an audible "beep." You'll locate it in seconds. Beep-N-Keep has a highly miniaturized sonic sensor which picks up your "signal" from up to 20' (6.1 m) away. It works even if the keys have fallen behind the couch, or are hidden under papers. You can attach them to other things to keep track of items as well, if desired. Don't drive yourself crazy trying to get out the door. **(I)**

PORTABLE ELECTRIC BABY SITTER

Another helpful home security device. If your youngster or elderly relative is sick, this voice-activated, wireless listening system lets you monitor their sounds from any location in the house. Young children occasionally get high fevers with hallucinations, or you may just want to listen in on their play time. Old people with heart conditions and strokes are a particular concern. Well, now there's no need to be neurotic and sit with them all the time. Don't neglect your chores and other household business. This transmitter has an omni-directional microphone, which picks up sounds from anywhere in a room and sends them back to a receiver by FM signal. Cries, children playing, or sick requests are easily heard, so you know your loved ones are safe. It plugs into any outlet. **(I)**

SOUND-ACTIVATED LIGHT SWITCH

Carrying heavy bags...or worried about home security when you arrive at night? Well, you can stop groping around for those hard-to-find light switches. The new Audiolite Plug turns on your lamps automatically at the sound of your voice or at the snap of a finger. With its sophisticated microchip circuitry, this sound-activated light switch can provide you with ease and security throughout your home. A built-in timer lets you adjust the intervals your lamps stay on—from seven seconds to seven minutes. Each new sound reactivates the internal mechanism to keep lights on without interruption. There's a manual switch for override as well. By placing Audiolite Plugs throughout your home you can help reduce utility bills and avoid potential break-ins. Turn off that robber by turning on unexpected light. **(I)**

PORTABLE DOOR ALARM

If you're worried about hotel-room security or you just want something simple to scare off potential prowlers, this device can do the job. It hangs on the inside of doors and sends out a piercing, eighty-five decibel alarm when jarred. A hand, key, credit card, or lock-picking tool sets it right off. Battery operated, its 4" (10.2 cm) diameter fits into any suitcase. **(I)**

ELECTRONIC FLYSWATTER

It's not for flies, but reportedly it does make the most difficult buzz sounds audible. This advanced PZM (Pressure Zone Microphone) uses a new method of recording whereby sound waves reinforce themselves in an area nearest a flat surface. So, by placing this special microphone in front of a conference or a choir, you get an even hemispherical pickup from every possible front angle. It's excellent for video recording, where planning for the sound direction is difficult. A singer or speaker can move away from the podium and you can be sure of capturing the voice. To better help you control a recording, the mike "buzzes off" all non-airborne sounds from the rear. It comes with a 10' (3.05 m) cord and one AA battery, good for up to six months. **(I)**

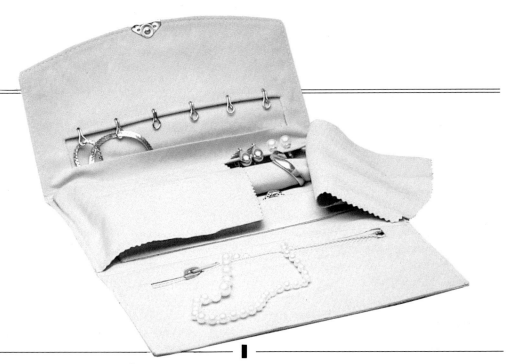

DRIVEWAY ALERT

Another home safety device for the paranoid soul. Do you know who's coming up your driveway? Driveway Alert is a twenty-four-hour early warning system to protect you and your family from potentially dangerous intruders. The very second a car passes over a special cable, Driveway Alert signals you, from up to 200' (61 m) away. Just place the transmitter stake into the ground next to your driveway. Extend the flexible 15' (4.6 m) signal cable across the driveway. The moment a vehicle treads on your turf, you'll be alerted. The transmitter uses a standard 9-volt battery that's included. The home receiver just plugs in. **(M)**

SENTRY SECURITY CHEST

Most people keep valuable documents at home. Insurance policies, tax records, single-copy manuscripts and the like are sometimes left scattered loosely around a house. But why take the chance of letting your whole life go up in smoke due to fire? Titles, beneficiaries, and other financial dealings could get tied up for years as a result. Rather than rent a safe-deposit box, invest in this Sentry Security Chest, reputed to withstand the ravages of fire. This portable insulated box is made of Pyronox to keep out the flames and heat. There are two sizes to accommodate a variety of items. Get that feeling of security in your own home. **(I)**

TRAVEL JEWELRY PROTECTOR

Americans travel more than ever these days. Whether backpacking or visiting St. Moritz, the problem of theft always exists when in unfamiliar territory. Hotel room robberies are a particular problem since an American passport today can bring over two thousand dollars on the black market. Rather than waste energy worrying about your valuables, the Travel Jewelry Protector can make your excursions more carefree. This compact, suede-finished pouch lets you secure bracelets, necklaces, and other items of value. Built-in hooks and snaps hold up to six pairs of earrings and up to five rings. A zippered pocket even affords room for credit cards or a wristwatch. Whether in town or on the go, carry your valuables with you. **(I)**

PHONE GUARD

Big brother got you down? Afraid of losing industrial secrets...or how about that ex-loved one trying to locate your assets? This inexpensive Phone Guard could be the answer to your communication security problem. It's a simple-to-install, advanced electronic device which attaches directly to your telephone. There's no need to spend a lot of money on detective agencies or expensive equipment. The Phone Guard alerts you instantly to any tap or bug on the line. The device replaces your telephone's existing mouthpiece but you speak normally. A bright red light tells you when someone's eavesdropping. It's even pocket-sized for mobile use. **(I)**

THE THINKING WALLET

Almost everyone has lost a bank or credit card due to theft or just plain carelessness. Well, here's a wallet that will help prevent the problem. If your card is missing after use, this special device alerts you with an electronic tone. Made with a standard sized thickness, the wallet's thin microcircuitry tells you that one of its six credit card slots is empty after you close it up. The top grade cowhide exterior hides two 1.5 volt silver batteries. The men's model is black with a 2½" (6.3 cm) slot for a notebook or checkbook. The burgundy women's model contains a 3¼" x 5¼" (8.25 x 13.33 cm) change purse, a special safety pocket, and an easily removable checkbook. **(I)**

CHALLENGER RECHARGEABLE FLOODLIGHT

It's not a standard flashlight, but is instead a powerful tool for special situations. Reportedly, the Challenger sends a beam of light that can be seen up to ¼ mi (402.39 m) away. Ever been stuck at sea with a dead engine or caught on a mountain with an approaching storm? People will have no trouble spotting you with this powerful floodlight by your side. Its Super 2 reflector comes in a weatherproof and waterproof case. It even floats in case you've capsized. It comes with two self-contained cords for recharging either from regular current or your car's battery. There's never a need to replace batteries, and it weighs less than 2 lbs (.908 kg) and is easy to store. **(I)**

TALKING WATCH

Space age technology comes down to earth. No more ridiculous gyrations with your arms to check the time. If you're carrying heavy items or driving with deliveries and need to know the time, just set this watch to continuously announce the time. Slow at getting to appointments? The device tells you to "hurry up" if you wish. You can even tell it to nag you like a snooze alarm. It will continue harassing every five minutes. There's half hour, minute, and second digital display. There's also a stopwatch with a lap counter and a day and date record. **(I)**

INTELLIGENT THERMOSTATS

You're coming home from a brutal day at the office. The humidity is ennervating. Wouldn't it be nice to come back to a cool apartment? With Intelligent Thermostats, you can. Whether in summer or in winter, this device will program your furnace or air conditioner to provide the temperature you want when you need it. It can hold six separate settings for one week so that you can program heat and cool air for any time of day. There's a manual override if things get a bit too sticky. This is a great money saver without costing you your comfort. An included isolation relay may be required for some homes and the unit won't work with two-stage furnace systems. **(I)**

HEAT SNIFFER

If your heating or air-conditioning bills are outrageously high, you may be victimized by unknown leaks and cracks in your house or apartment. Just turn this unit on and adjust for silence. Move the Sniffer's sensor along walls and window frames and other structures. Changes in the temperature set off a beeping alarm and a flashing LCD. It's effective in temperatures from 59°–95°F (15 °–35 °C). A 9-volt battery is required. (I)

LIGHT ALERT

A great outdoor security device. This unit scares off crooks before they even come close. Control the perimeter of your house by flooding its grounds with bright light. A sophisticated, heat-detecting infrared sensor picks up any approaching car or person from up to 40' (12.19 m) away. The Light Alert then turns on its adjustable beams for ten seconds, or up to ten minutes. It's a great energy saver when you come home late at night and don't want to stumble around in the dark. No need to leave lights burning all the time. The device will help you move around, and also frighten off those prowlers or pranksters. It comes with two weatherproof floodlight sockets, a sensor, and the junction box. If you already have exterior lighting, the sensor can be purchased separately. You'll never be surprised in the dark. (M)

NUTONE WIRELESS DOOR CHIME

An important delivery is coming but you're afraid to do that work up in the attic and miss the doorbell. It's a familiar story. Many people postpone important chores in their basement, backyard, or attic, just to make sure they hear the doorbell ring.

No longer. With this new wireless door chime, you can be sure to know when company is calling. With NuTone, the doorbell's chime is transmitted by radio waves to any location up to 100' (30.5 m) away—indoors or out. There are no wires. Just attach the push-button transmitter outside your door. When a visitor pushes the button, your receiver activates a pleasant chime. It can even be used as a warning device for the elderly or an invalid. Sit by your pool, or take care of business...you'll know when someone is knocking. (I)

BOOK-SAFE

If your house has been broken into, you know the emotional trauma of losing valuables. Sometimes it's not even the television or other large items we miss but the family rings and small heirlooms that have more sentimental value. Unfortunately, crooks can't discriminate and instead grab everything in sight. With this Book-Safe, you can hide your special jewelry, important papers, and cash inside the false binding. The cut-out-cavity is about 8"x 5"x 1¼" (20.3 x 13 x 3.17 cm), so it's large enough to hold a number of items. Any good crook can quickly crack a safe, but few of them will stop to read through your library. Each book is so inconspicuous, you may have trouble locating it unless you memorize the title. If you work in an office where things seem to slip off your desk whenever you walk away, don't waste time locking them up. Do it by the book. **(I)**

KEY STONE

A great idea. Most people who live in private houses leave an extra key somewhere near the perimeter. It's usually under the mat, above a ledge, or in some other relatively accessible location. Robbers know this and are most adept at figuring out your hiding spot. Not with this Key Stone. It looks and feels just like any ordinary garden rock that can sit under a bush, along your walk, or in a flower bed. But once you turn it over, inside is a secret compartment that can hold up to four spare keys. Using a knife you can create even more room. A sliding cover keeps away the bugs. **(C)**

BLAZE-OUT FIRE EXTINGUISHER

This is a great little helper if you occasionally have grease fires or other small blazes. Fire experts recommend you keep a fire extinguisher in trouble spots like the basement and kitchen. But those large metal units can be an eyesore. This small vial uses Halon 1211, the same colorless and odorless agent racing car crews apply to stop fires immediately. It's effective on all kinds of fires and can work from up to 9' (2.745 m) away. There's no messy residue unlike chemical or foam extinguishers. It weighs less than 1 lb (.454 kg) and comes with a clip for carrying and a bracket for wall mounting. Remove the safety ring and aim. The Halon gas snuffs out oxygen. **(C)**

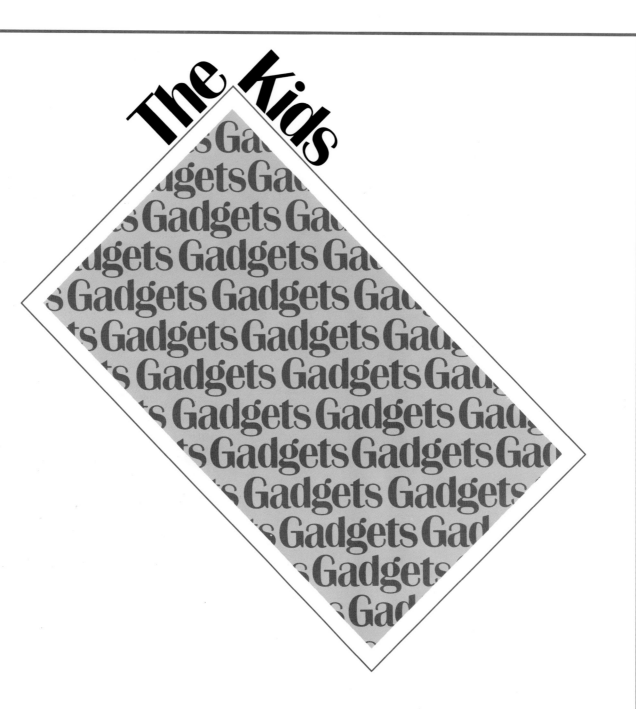

The Kids' Gadgets

■

COMPUTERIZED PIGGY BANK

Remember the old days? You'd take what money was left over from your allowance and put it into that oversized piggy bank until it burst. Not any longer. Now your kids can get the same old-fashioned enjoyment of putting away money for a rainy day while learning the fundamentals of modern banking. This combined calcu-lator-piggy bank notes all deposits and withdrawals and remembers on-going balance in up to eight digits. Teach them good savings habits at an early age, while they develop business so-phistication. There are two keys to open the vault so you can control your chil-dren's spending habits at the same time and teach them an important skill. **(I)**

■

DELUXE SAFETY SITTER

Parents are always wor-ried about their little one in the tub. You really do have to be careful about drowning when they're at a certain age. But with this helpful device, you can rush to answer the phone or do another quick nearby chore without fear of fatal-ity. The Deluxe Sitter helps keep your kid safely seated in the bathtub. Made of sturdy plastic, it attaches with four gi-ant suction cups to prevent active tots from toppling it. It comes with a cushy, no-slip contoured seat, and is perfect for kiddies from six to thirty months old. **(I)**

■

AMPHIBIAN 110 UNDERWATER CAMERA

The kids will love to dive down with this great device. When we think of underwater photography, we think of expensive equipment or crews filming in tanks. Well now we can enjoy that same thrill of photo-graphing and viewing deep sea photos. Going on a family trip to some island? Take this magnificent device along and those exotic fish you saw while snorkel-ing won't be just a memory. It's tiny enough to slip into the pocket of your diving gear if you're going down deep. Or, just swim in shallow depths and snap. However you dive, the device can withstand depths of up to 160' (48.77 m). Best of all, it's simple to operate. Just aim and shoot like today's auto-matic land models. The Amphibian's automatic motor drive advances the film at one frame per second. There's a mechanical shutter with a safety lock set at 125th of a second. The F4 wide-angle lens is pre-focused. There's even a built-in electronic flash with an LED low-light warning to let you know. You purchase the two "AA" alkaline batter-ies for power. Bring the mysteries of the deep right into your own home with this fun and easy-to-use gadget. **(E)**

PRENATAL-SOUND LAMB

There are many ways to soothe a crying baby but the best and most effective method comes from the mother. While in the womb, the fetus hears certain soothing sounds. During birth and in infancy, a baby is assaulted with new noises that can be frightening and disturbing. This pacifier, developed by the noted obstetrician Dr. William C. Eller, reproduces the actual sounds heard inside the womb of an expectant mother and has been proven effective in hospital tests. This lamb contains a transistorized, battery-operated miniature amplifier and speaker which electronically reproduce the recorded sounds. An exceptional way to quiet crying babies and lull them to sleep, the Prenatal-Sound Lamb is also fire retardant and non-allergenic. The eyes are fastened securely with washers and cannot be pulled off; the on/off knob is capable of withstanding twenty-five pounds of pull. The lamb is easily washable, too. The pocket that holds the sound unit has a Velcro flap so that the unit can be taken out and the lamb washed. The lamb is 11" (27.94 cm) high. For babies who prefer teddy bears, a Prenatal-Sound Teddy Bear is also available. (I)

SAFETY BATH WHALE

It's been said that a majority of childhood accidents happen in the bath tub. Taking a bath can be playtime fun for most kids, but playing while bathing can lead to accidents. One of the most obvious areas of concern is the water spout in the tub. Many times, kids will slip and bump their heads against the protruding tub spout—sometimes seriously, sometimes not. Using this adorable great white whale is an easy way to prevent a serious accident. Made of cushioned rubber, it slips easily over the bathtub spout and can be snugly secured with two adjustable straps. The Safety Bath Whale is split down the top to accommodate shower control levers. Add an imaginative spark to bathtime without skimping on safety. **(C)**

SOCKET LOCK-IT

The moment baby starts to crawl can be a thrilling time for parents, but it is also a time to take extra safety precautions. Babies love to explore and investigate their surroundings, and will poke, pull, and probe everything within reach. Many parents take special measures to insure that nothing harmful is nearby. The electrical wall socket, however, is a forgotten item that almost always provokes the curiosity of babies, toddlers, and small children. The Socket Lock-It was designed to thwart small fingers from examining dangerous electrical outlets. This unique device has two spring-loaded doors that only adults can manipulate. These doors automatically snap closed when a plug is removed. It's 4" (10.16 cm) long and simple to install—a must for every safety-conscious parent. **(C)**

The Office Gadgets

WORLD CLOCK

If you frequently do business on the telephone, this clock is a great device to help close that deal. At a glance, the World Clock tells you the time anywhere around the globe. Just set it for your own time zone and the dial displays local time like a regular clock. Using the recessed time scale, you can instantly scan the globe to figure out the time zone for any city you want. The elegant, brushed-brass case comes with a 7" (17.8 cm) gold/bronze dial. They'll know you mean business when they see the World Clock on your desk. **(M)**

THE ONLY FOLDING PRINTING CALCULATOR

It comes with a full-sized keyboard and a printer. This folding calculator easily fits into a jacket pocket or purse. The device performs all basic calculator functions and reportedly is forty-one percent thinner than other hand held printing calculators. It has four-key memory, in addition to keys for percent, non-add print, square root, sign change, clear entry, and paper advance. A 1½" (3.8 cm) wide thermal paper is included. Additional rolls must be ordered extra. An AC adapter is also an additional expense. **(I)**

CASIO CREDIT CARD CALCULATOR

Everyone uses a calculator today, but here's one that's as small and thin as your credit cards. If you are a nut for checking the bill at a restaurant, just pretend to be shuffling for credit cards in your wallet. Promptly add up the bill without feeling foolish for making people wait around for you to manually total your meal. It looks just like a major credit card, only 1/32" of an inch thick. But the best thing is that it requires no batteries. Room light, sunlight, any kind of light, powers this unique credit card calculator. It performs four basic functions plus memory, square root, sign change, and percent key with an LCD display. **(I)**

ELECTRONIC DICTIONARY TYPEWRITER

Every office has some wordprocessing system these days. But the time it takes to chose the right hardware and learn the software may be too much for smaller outfits or individual entrepreneurs. If you need something for prompt typing, but want the wordprocessing features of more sophisticated machines, this new Smith-Corona electronic typewriter may be just right. It comes with a built-in spelling checker containing the roots of 35,000 words, more than many computer software dictionaries. If you type a misspelled word while working, the machine signals the mistake with a "beep" tone. The unit then helps find and correct the error and then returns to your place in the text. Impressive? There's more. This state-of-the-art typewriter has features like end-of-page warning system, automatic return and centering, and automatic underscoring. It offers dual pitch print in ten or twelve characters per inch, and can change typefaces by dropping in another daisy wheel. Programmable tabs, margins, and express backspace help you get started quickly. Take the fear out of typing errors without making a dent in your wallet. **(E)**

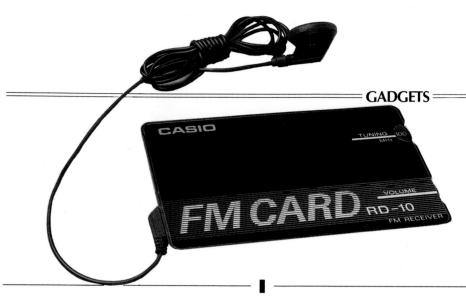

CASIO CARD RADIO

There are plenty of small radios made today but, reportedly, this is the slimmest, lightest unit in the world. It's only the size of a credit card so you can carry it around in your wallet. Need to check up on current news or financial information? This model makes it easy. Advanced miniaturization technology has reduced the required radio circuitry into tiny IC circuits. You can even design the Card Radio's exterior. Put on your company logo, individual monogram, or favorite motif. An excellent gift item. **(I)**

STOCK MARKET MONITOR

Now you can stay on top of that portfolio without fear. If you move around frequently for business but still like to call the investment shots, this device will keep you instantaneously informed of the most up-to-the-minute stock price quotations. There's no delay. It's like being on the trading floor itself. The device can store up to forty security symbols that you program. If you request a quote on another symbol not in memory, the data is only delayed two to seventy seconds. The unit receives high-speed digital data broadcasts on a private FM band via satellite to cities across the country. The coverage includes the New York and American Stock Exchanges, NASDAQ, Chicago Board of Trade, Chicago Mercantile Exchange and the CEC. If you live within a fifty mile radius of broadcasting centers in New York, Chicago, Dallas, Los Angeles, or San Francisco, you are in business. Other cities will become available shortly. Request data from your stock's last sale, net change, high, low, open or close, and total volume. It's easy to read with the unit's forty character, LCD readout. Of course there is a subscription fee, so ask before you order. The device runs on a rechargeable silver-zinc battery pack. **(E)**

COMMAND DIALER PHONE

Welcome to the future! This ingenious device is, reportedly, the world's first voice activated telephone with the ability to store, retrieve, and automatically dial numbers at the sound of your voice. State-of-the-art microprocessor technology lets you program up to sixteen regularly called numbers by saying a preselected code name. Just mention that special loved one, or your place of business, verbally confirm the number by saying "dial," and they're on the line in seconds. The machine automatically redials if the number's busy. Once you're talking, a speaker phone allows for hand-free communication. The system even recognizes different voices, so your entire family can use it. Comes with built-in alarm clock and a battery to prevent losing programmed numbers in case of power failures. **(M)**

REPRO 2000

This machine is perfect if you're a small businessperson or individual entrepreneur. If you need an occasional copy but like the convenience of not having to go out just to make a record, why spend unnecessarily to lease a large Xerox or copy machine? At $39.95, this Repro 2000 is just what you need. The manufacturer claims that its quality is comparable to costlier machines but is a fraction of the cost. They are so confident that there's a thirty-day trial period. You can get a complete refund if you're not satisfied. The device comes with developer and some paper. **(I)**

EASYTALK HEADSET HEADBAND

Do you frequently do several different things at once while working at your desk? It's difficult for most people to talk on the phone while doing paperwork at the same time. If you take or look up orders, need to give price information, or are so swamped you must type and talk on the telephone at the same time, then this hands-free phone headset can really help you get the job done. Just plug the modular jack into your phone base and the EasyTalk lets you perform a variety of functions without grappling with that receiver. Both the headset and your original receiver plug into the unit's amplifier, so you can switch from headset to headset without any trouble. It's basically a civilian version of what astronauts, phone operators, and pilots use. Forget struggling with the hard plastic against your ear. This device offers you a soft foam ear cushion so that you can go about your business. Note...there's also an headband model so specify when ordering. **(I)**

AUTOMATIC PAPER SHREDDER

You don't have to belong to the CIA to want to destroy records. Industrial espionage is a big problem today. A number of cases have reported competitors hunting through garbage to obtain trade secrets. If you work on highly confidential material or are an entrepreneur in a developing industry, you may be concerned about the janitorial team roaming the building. Just pick up this Automatic Paper Shredder and you'll sleep soundly once again. Reportedly, it's the only machine that adjusts to fit any size wastebasket—round, square, or rectangular. Most shredders take up an entire receptacle. Not this unit. It's small enough to allow for both shredded and unshredded material, and to be removed and stored easily when not in use. The machine can handle almost any kind of material. Hard-end, steel blades cut through computer cards, film negatives, and all types of paper. A contoured feed opening makes hand guiding unnecessary. Extendable mounting from 12½" to 17½" (31.8 to 44.4 cm). Don't go crazy over discarded documents when you can count on this shredder for a quick and easy clean up. **(M)**

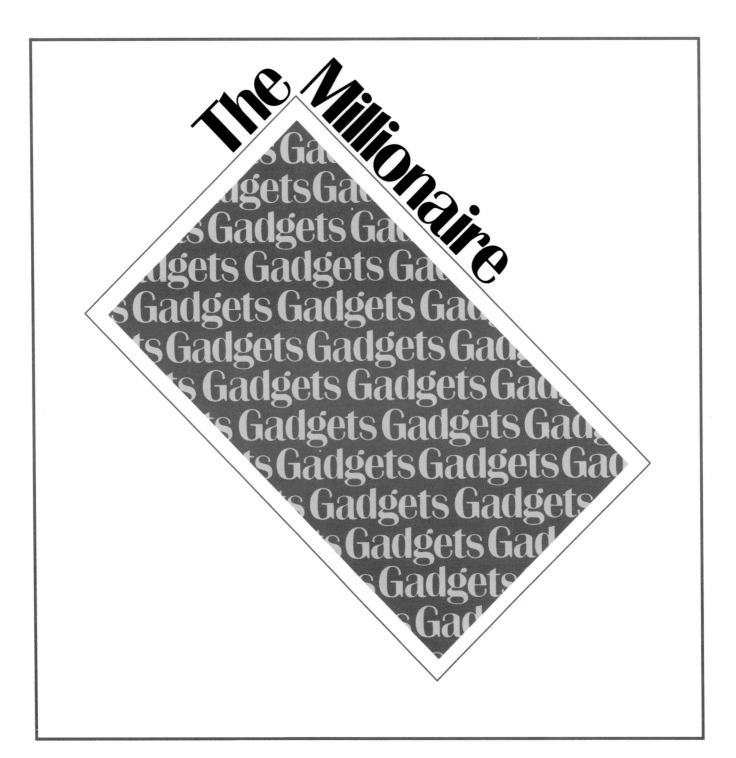

The Millionaire Gadgets

SECRET CONNECTION BRIEFCASE

James Bond never had it so good. This state-of-the-art security device contains the most sophisticated systems known today. Some of the equipment can even be found on AWACS spy planes. In operation, many of the devices are disguised as regular items. Worried about getting caught in a bribe or bad deal? There's a cigarette case pack which lights up when tape recorders are present. An ordinary pen illuminates when a "bug" is around. And there's a sniffer to detect hidden bombs. You know your corporate president will feel much safer in that volatile third-world country with this attaché case nearby. The unit also has offensive capabilities. There's a flashlight at your fingertips designed to blind evildoers for up to four hours with an intense beam of light. Trying to close a deal, or hunt down terrorists? A wireless telephone with a built-in scambler lets you coordinate communications. The handy voice-stress analyzer reveals whether the party you're speaking to is telling the truth. Under direct attack? Use the briefcase as a shield. Its rough synthetic fabric will withstand a .359 magnum bullet. If someone tries to steal the briefcase, an alarm will sound for six seconds after the case is ripped from the owner's grasp. It weighs 22 lbs (9.98 kg) fully loaded. Look out...007. **(I)**

STROKE SAVER

Beat the boys back at the club. With this device, they'll wonder what happened to your game. This Stroke Saver finds a golf ball's exact center of gravity. If you hit it there, the ball will go farther and straighter. It uses centrifugal force to locate the exact gravity center. Just push the button and the ball spins around to a stop. Mark the top spot for a guide and yell "fore." **(I)**

ENGLISH PUTTER FLASK

A nip of your favorite spirit while you have fun on the green? You and your golfing partner may have some trouble by the eighteenth hole, but no one will be complaining. If that Sunday morning golf game has become a little too staid, spice it up with this Putter Flask before lunch. The club will never know. Inside the steel shaft is a flask that holds 3.38 oz (100 ml) of whatever you're drinking. It's a well-balanced center putter with a solid brass head. But don't let it get to you when you drive home. **(I)**

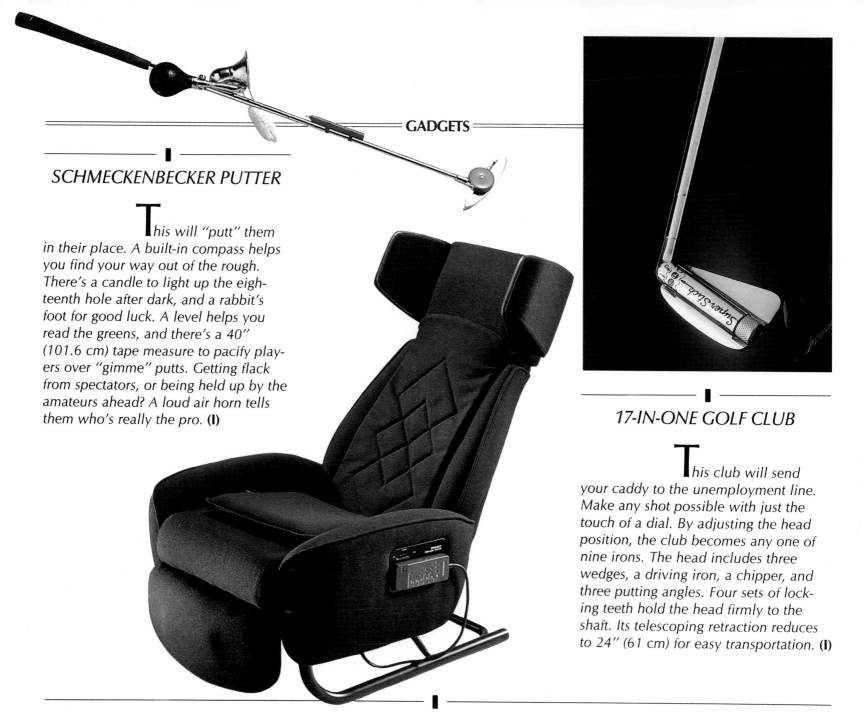

SCHMECKENBECKER PUTTER

This will "putt" them in their place. A built-in compass helps you find your way out of the rough. There's a candle to light up the eighteenth hole after dark, and a rabbit's foot for good luck. A level helps you read the greens, and there's a 40" (101.6 cm) tape measure to pacify players over "gimme" putts. Getting flack from spectators, or being held up by the amateurs ahead? A loud air horn tells them who's really the pro. **(I)**

17-IN-ONE GOLF CLUB

This club will send your caddy to the unemployment line. Make any shot possible with just the touch of a dial. By adjusting the head position, the club becomes any one of nine irons. The head includes three wedges, a driving iron, a chipper, and three putting angles. Four sets of locking teeth hold the head firmly to the shaft. Its telescoping retraction reduces to 24" (61 cm) for easy transportation. **(I)**

OSAKA ELECTRIC MASSAGE/STEREO CHAIR

State-of-the-art relaxation. This microprocessor-driven massage chair contains a built-in AM/FM stereo and cassette player. Your tensions will fade away as the machine's two massage rollers revive tired and aching muscles to the sounds of your favorite music or information programming. With a built-in timer, adjustable controls help you focus in on knots and energy blocks for as long as it takes. Three separate motors also provide massage for your back and legs. For comfort, this special chair adjusts easily from its upright position to a near-prone position. Speakers are built into three-position, swiveling, wrap-around panels at the head, so you get maximum stereo imaging. A relaxing sound effects tape is included containing soothing bird calls, running water, and an ocean surf. **(VE)**

TRAVELING STEREO ATTACHÉ

Only the very rich or music enthusiasts will spring for this one. We've all been on the road and suddenly gotten the urge for our favorite album. Many people carry portable cassette decks, but the tape hiss played through inferior speakers is not up to snuff. Headphones are okay, but what about that intimate hotel tryst for two? This compact Stereo Attaché case will blend into any first-class suite. It's a completely portable entertainment system with a built-in stereo cassette recorder, a record player with a 7" (17.8 cm) turntable, and a four-band AM/FM/SW1/SW2 radio for use at home and abroad. Two 5" (12.7) speakers each have four feet of speaker wire that can be separated for acceptable stereo imaging. There's a condenser microphone if you need to dictate notes to yourself or want a kinky record of that night in bliss. The Attaché can run on either 110 or 220 volts and even D batteries. **(E)**

GOLF 'N' GO II

It's really two bags in one. The outer bag is a weather-proof storage unit that holds everything you'll need for that get-away golf weekend. No need to cut down on clothing because you can't carry two separate bags. The inside unit is a three-pound, lightweight bag that holds all the equipment you'll ever carry to make that tough chip shot. Clubs, balls, shoes, and tees ease inside the various fitted compartments. There's a removable rain hood and a detachable "sherpa" carrying strap. Both bags are made from a tough high-density DuPont cordura fabric. Swing into action. **(M)**

THE ASCOT UMBRELLA SEAT-STICK

This English acquisition is standard for the upper-crust. They use it at Ascot and other equestrian events, boat races, golf tournaments, or while hunting or fishing for trout and salmon. The versatile walking seat-stick doubles as an umbrella. It lets you lean or stand comfortably for long periods with class, while observing or playing in sporting events. An aluminum shaft rests securely on the ground-plate for stability while leaning or walking. A foam padded pigskin seat is attached to the aluminum handles that turn the seat into compact umbrella handles for those inclement weather days. Cheerio . . . ! **(I)**

THE WORLD'S ONLY COMPUTERIZED FISHING REEL

Don't let this one get away. It's a unique fishing reel that comes with a microcomputer to tell you exactly how you're casting. The LCD readout shows the amount of line you've used and what remains after a cast, and tells when you're trolling. It lets you know every second that your lure is sinking by a beep sound so that you can hit that same spot. The reel then displays your retrieve speed in feet-per-second on a bar graph, as you try to attract and then pull in the tough catch. The reel has a blacklash control, a zero-friction line guide and uses ball bearings for smoother action. It weighs only 8.6 oz (243.81 g), just slightly more than comparable non-electric models. The line capacity is 199 yds (181.886 m) using 8, 10, or 12 lb (3.63, 4.5, or 5.45 kg) test. **(M)**

CHESALTURF PUTTING GREEN

Practice that putt right in your own home. Most artificial practice surfaces do not duplicate the feeling of a real putting green. This special, deep-textured, artificial turf actually simulates the putting surface, giving you a realistic impression of speed, line, and slope. Four inch (10.2 cm) cups are ¼" (.635 cm) smaller than regulation size, so you can improve your shot by overcoming the challenge. The holes are set off from each other to test you with different angles. It's 9' (2.745 m) long, with a slight incline at the end to improve your abilities. Rolls up easily to store in your closet. **(I)**

SOLAR-POWERED VENTILATED PITH HELMET

Taking an African safari or thinking of exploring some ancient desert city? You can protect yourself from the sun and stay cool at the same time with this solar-powered, ventilated pith helmet. A built-in fan directs a constant breeze toward your forehead to cool you on a hot day. Six ½-volt solar cells on top power the motor with sunlight, while a battery under the brim runs the helmet at night. If it's really steaming, just moisten the perforated sponge that attaches by a velcro strip to the adjustable headband inside. As the water evaporates on your forehead, you cool off. Varnished mesh construction provides ventilation and protection from the sun. Only 8 oz. **(I)**

Travel
Gadgets

TRAVEL CLOCK AND SMOKE ALARM

This is no ordinary travel clock. This unique combination will make sure that you wake up on time and will sound a warning signal in case of fire. Many hotel rooms are ill-equipped with modern safety features. Why not be as safe in your hotel as you are in your home? The clock has a wake-up alarm and luminous hands for reading the time in the dark. The detachable smoke alarm is fitted with a bracket that will hang over any door. Just to be sure, the alarm also includes a test button. When the clock and smoke detector are snapped together the whole piece takes up only 5¼″ x 2⅜″ x 1⅛″ (3 x 6 x 3 cm³). Light and perfectly portable, no smart traveler should be without this duo. The complete clock and alarm set is powered by a 9-volt and one AA battery. **(I)**

CORDLESS, COMPACT TRAVEL LAMP

This brilliantly designed travel lamp is the only portable lamp that enables you to read anywhere. It's cordless, compact and folds perfectly to fit into small spaces such as a briefcase or purse. If you are in a situation that affords little or no light, or if you forgot to bring an electrical adaptor abroad, this lamp will save the day. It uses a special, soft-light flourescent bulb instead of the harsh, glaring incandescent bulbs found in most lamps and casts a glare-free light that will reduce eye strain and provide for easy, comfortable reading. The lamp will give you ninety continuous minutes of light on a ten-hour charge of the four 1.2 volt batteries. Optional AC adapter is also available. The 4-watt battery recharger plugs into any household outlet. Unfolded, the lamp is 11¼" (28 cm) high and weighs 16.8 ounces (523 g). **(I)**

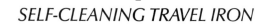

SELF-CLEANING TRAVEL IRON

Reportedly, the only travel steam iron with a setting that lets it clean itself after each use. The distributor claims it also has twice the water capacity of other travel irons. The iron can be operated horizontally for dry and steam pressing, or vertically for steam-burst ironing. Adjustable temperature controls can handle all fabrics. It weighs only 1½ lbs (.68 kg), and the foldable handle makes it easy for transportation. There's dual voltage for international use.**(I)**

INTERNATIONAL TRAVELER'S CONVERTER KIT

Tired of going to foreign hotels and having to rent an electrical converter? Don't want to wait in line at that small pension just to be able to dry your hair? With this complete converter unit you can use your hair dryer, razor, radio, or other electric appliances anywhere in the world. The dual case contains two converters for both 110-volt and 220-volt appliances. There's also a high-wattage converter for using razors, radios, etc. The five adapter plugs are color-keyed to coordinate with the world map that is also included. They match the various electrical type outlets around the globe. **(I)**

TRAVELER'S WATER HEATER

You can have an instant cup of tea, coffee or soup anywhere in the world with this traveler's water heater. Instead of using room service, it's easier, quicker, and less expensive to make your own soothing refreshment. This convenient device is made to last and travel as long as you do. It operates on a 110- or 220-volt current and comes with an adapter plug for foreign outlets. A sleek travel case helps the heater fit easily into your suitcase, briefcase or pocketbook. Just slip the heater into a cup of water and you'll be ready for that cup of coffee. **(C)**

Sources

ABERCROMBIE AND FITCH
2300 Maxwell Lane
Houston, Tex. 77023
800 231-9715

AUSTIN-ABBOTT INC.
202 S. First Avenue
Highland Park, N.J. 08904

BIALETTI-IPE CORP.
Box 180A Albany Post Road
Garrison, N.Y. 10524
914 424-4133

BOODABOX PRODUCTS
439 S. Detroit Street
Los Angeles, Calif. 90036

BROOKSTONE
648 Vose Farm Road
Peterborough, N.H. 03458

CAN DO
750 N. Milford Road
Highland, Md. 48031
313 887-7454

CASIO
15 Gardner Road
Fairfield, N.J. 07006

CCS COMMUNICATIONS CONTROL INC.
633 Third Avenue
New York, N.Y. 10017
212 697-8140

CITY CORP DINERS CLUB
DINERS CHOICE
125 Armstrong Road
Des Plaines, Ill. 60018
800 621-1268

CUISINE CONCEPTS NORDIC WARE
Hiway 7
Minneapolis, Minn. 55416

DAK INDUSTRIES
8200 Remmet Avenue
Canoga Park, Calif. 91304
800 325-0800

DELMART-DELUXE CHECK PRINTERS
2199 N. Pascal
P.O. Box 64495
St. Paul, Minn. 55164-0495
800 328-9697

DYNAMIC DIRECT
Box 5026
New Hyde Park, N.Y. 11040
800 228-2323

EQUITY INDUSTRIES
5721 Bayside Road
Virginia Beach, Va. 23455
804 460-2483

EXECUTIVE CORNER
62 Greenpoint Avenue
Brooklyn, N.Y. 11222
800 431-9003

EXETERS
3303 Harbor Boulevard
Suite B-5
Costa Mesa, Calif. 92926
800 525-4477

FITCH CREATIONS
Box 111
Chapel Hill, N.C. 27514
919 942-5107

FLEXPORT-TUREN INC.
Etna Road
Lebanon, N.H. 03766
603 448-2990

FOLEY BELSAW
6301 Equitable Road
P.O. Box 593
Kansas City, Mo. 64141
800 821-3452

FOX RUN CRAFTMAN
Polinski Road
P.O. Box 2727
Ivyland, Pa. 18974
215 675-7700

HAMMACHER SCHLEMMER & CO.
16 East 57th Street
New York, N.Y. 10022
800 368-3564

HANDY INDUSTRIES
P.O. Box 2456
Jonesboro, Ak. 72401
501 932-9213

HEATHKIT
Benton Harbor, Mich. 49022
800 253-0570

HONEX CORP.
3000 Sand Hill Road
Menlo Park, Calif. 94025
800 227-3800 Ex. 47916

INNOVATIONS
110 Painters Mill Road
Owing Mills, Md. 21117
800 638-6130

JOYCE CHEN PRODUCTS FOR
HOME & KITCHEN
411 Waverly Oaks Road
Waltham, Mass. 02154
617 643-1930

LILLIAN VERNON
520 South Fulton Avenue
Mount Vernon, N.Y. 10550
914 633-6300

MISS KIMBALL OF OSHKOSH
41 West 8th Avenue
Oshkosh, Wis. 54901

ROWOCO INC.
Building 4 Warehouse Lane Road
Elmsford, N.Y. 10523
800 431-2658

SOUTHWEST LABS
3505 Cadillac Avenue
Building F1
Costa Mesa, Calif. 92626
714 549-0959

TOYS TO GROW ON
2695 E. Dominquez Street
P.O. Box 17
Long Beach, Calif. 90801
213 603-8890

WEBCOR ELECTRONICS
107 Charles Lindbergh Boulevard
Garden City, N.Y. 11530
516 794-6200

WILLIAM SONOMA
P.O. Box 7456
San Francisco, Calif. 94120
415 652-1515

WINEKEEPER
423 N. Quarantina Street
Santa Barbara, Calif. 93101
805 963-3451

ROOM-BY-ROOM GUIDE TO SUPPLIERS

THE KITCHEN

BROOKSTONE:
Microwave Tester
Professional Chef's
Thermometer
FLEXPORT, TUREN INC.:
Flexport, Various Model Sizes
HAMMACHER SCHLEMMER:
Cabinet Jar Opener
Cape Cod Oyster and Clam
Openers
Cordless Electric Pepper Mill
Cordless Food Warmer
Electric Ice Cream Scoop
Electric Pasta Maker
Electric Self Stirring Sauce Pan
La Valtromplina Nut and Bean
Roaster
Portable Mini-Stove
Self Chilling Butter Dish
Three-In-One Buffet Utensil
World's Only Cordless Electric
Carving Knife
HONEX CORP.:
Mug Mate
INNOVATIONS:
Toastless Electric Kettle
LILLIAN VERNON:
Garlic Jar
Oil and Vinegar Server
ROWOCO INC.:
Pull Top Opener
WILLIAM SONOMA:
Tomato Press

THE PANTRY

BOODABOX PRODUCTS:
Boodabox Odor Free Litter Box
HAMMACHER SCHLEMMER:
Compucal Nutrition Computer
Gaggia Electric Distiller
INNOVATIONS:
Kool Mate

THE DINING ROOM

AUSTIN-ABBOTT INC.:
Plate-Mate
HAMMACHER SCHLEMMER:
Electric Plate Blanket
Oshibori Hot Towel Basket
Sonic Silver Cleaner

THE BAR

EXETERS:
Portable Wine Wizard
HAMMACHER SCHLEMMER:
Folding Instant Bar
The Thermo-Vinometer
World's Best Corkscrew
WINEKEEPER:
Winekeeper

THE LIVING ROOM

DAK INDUSTRIES:
Air Easy Pollution Shield
EXETERS:
Hands Free Speakerphone
HAMMACHER SCHLEMMER:
Efficiency Fireplace Heat
Recycler
HANDY INDUSTRIES:
Gourmet Nutcracker
INNOVATIONS:
The Button
Initech 3100P Phone Answering
System
Singing Telephone
Smokeaway Smokeless
Electronic Ashtray
SOUTHWEST LABS:
Chimney Fire Extinguisher

THE BEDROOM

EXETERS:
Marsona Sound Conditioner
HAMMACHER SCHLEMMER:
Heat Sensing Automatic Blanket
Safe-Escape Instant Portable
Ladder
INNOVATIONS:
Intelliphone
Magnavox Clock/Audio/
Communications Center

THE CLOSETS

BROOKSTONE:
Electronically Heated Socks and
Mittens
Non-Electric Dehumidifier
HAMMACHER SCHLEMMER:
The Hideaway Ironing Center
INNOVATIONS:
Extendable Belt & Tie Rack
Pants Presser Valet

THE UTILITY ROOM

BROOKSTONE:
Long Burning Candle
Pet Washer
Retractable Dog Leash
HAMMACHER SCHLEMMER:
Aria Light Socket Fan
Automatic Pet Watering System
Double Buffer Electric Shoe
Polisher
Floating Stereo
The Gabbot Double Umbrella
Magnetic Window Cleaner
Miniature Folding Umbrella
Stake-Down Inflatable Headrest
Beach Towel
INNOVATIONS:
Computemp 3
Temperature/Clock
The Currency Exchanger
Billfold
Electronic Flea Collar
Electrosonic Jewelry Cleaner
Mini-Vac
Pest-Pruff II
Survivor 15-Function Tool
Xtralite
MISS KIMBALL OF OSHKOSH:
Urine Kleen

THE PLAYROOM AND THE DEN

BROOKSTONE:
Telephone Hearing Amplifier
DAK INDUSTRIES:
Remote Control Watch
HAMMACHER SCHLEMMER:
The Ceiling Projector Clock
Computerized Home
Meteorological Station
Home Video Printer
Las Vegas One-Armed Bandit
"Monte"—Computer Scrabble
Master
Phone Activated Stereo Silencer
The Talking Computer Bridge
Player
The 360° Panoramic Camera
The Voice Deactivated Alarm
Clock
INNOVATIONS:
Alpha 8 Translator

Chess King Pocket Micro
Citizen Chronograph/Stopwatch
Cordless Stereo Headphones
Holmes Air Ultrasonic
Humidifier
Remote Controller for
VHF/UHF
Ver-bot Voice Activated Robot
MISS KIMBALL OF OSHKOSH:
100 Year Night Light

THE EXERCISE ROOM

BROOKSTONE:
Grip Exerciser
DAK INDUSTRIES:
Portable Heart Window
EXETERS:
Automatic Digitronic
Pedio Massager
HAMMACHER SCHLEMMER:
Bennett's Bend Tennis Racquet
Digital Jog and Walk Pedometer
The Freestanding Wet/Dry
Sauna
Health Club Rowing Machine
Personal Calorie
Monitor/Computer
Scullers Ergometer
Tachikawa Full Body Massage
Machine
INNOVATIONS:
Accu-Vibe Massager
Run-Alert

THE BATHROOM

BROOKSTONE:
Gyroscopic Razor
HAMMACHER SCHLEMMER:
The English Heated Towel Stand
The Home Water Still
Illuminated Multi-Angle
Extension Mirror
Novus Digital Bathroom Scale
Only Talking Scale With
Memory
The Shower Radio
Whirlpool Bathtub Converter
INNOVATIONS:
Electronic Thermometer
The Groomsman II
Hands-Free Shower Phone II
Heated Toilet Seat
Infralux

Wet Duet Pulsating Shower Massage

MISS KIMBALL OF OSHKOSH:
Rotary Nose Hair Clipper

THE WORKROOM

BROOKSTONE:
Aerator Sandals
Equal-Arm Boring Hole
Glue Injector
High Reach Chain Saw
Perfboard Containers
Precision Oiler
Sonic Ear Valves
Supersensitive Water Alarm

FITCH CREATIONS:
Corner Clip System

HAMMACHER SCHLEMMER:
Double Wedge Electric Log Splitter

INNOVATIONS:
Calcutape
Flexladder
Handi-Hook
Insta Pump
Log Press
Power-Flow Roller Painting System
Stud Sensor

THE GREENHOUSE

BROOKSTONE:
PH Meter
Saw/Pruner
Soil Analysis Gauge
Three Automatic Waterers
Ultrasonic Bird Discourager

CAN DO:
Can-Do Digger

HAMMACHER SCHLEMMER:
Nellors Garden SeedFeeder
The World's Only Rolling Gardener's Seat

INNOVATIONS:
Rainmatic

JOYCE CHEN PRODUCTS FOR HOME & KITCHEN:
Zip-it-Open Instant Bag Opener

THE PATIO AND THE PORCH

BROOKSTONE:
Automatic Light Switch
Charcoal Starter
Mail Alert
Pet Fountain

EXETERS:
New Lavastone Barbecue

HAMMACHER SCHLEMMER:
Reflecting Suntan Mat
Squirrel Resistant Bird Feeder
The Sun-Tracking Four Position Beach Chair
Tan-O-Meter

INNOVATIONS:
Aqualume Moonlight
Bionic Ear
Citizen Pocket TV
Deluxe Pool Alarm System
Patio Hose and Reel
Sunmist
Swirlon Rotary Washer Scrubber
Tele-Ranger

WEBER ELECTRONICS:
Float Phone

THE GARAGE AND THE CAR

BROOKSTONE:
Flexstand Rope Tow
Headlight Reminder
Instant Spare Tire Inflator
Map Meter

EXETERS:
Carbon Monoxide Detector
Charge It

HAMMACHER SCHLEMMER:
Adjustable Lumbar Massaging Seatback
Remote Car Starter

INNOVATIONS:
Car Finder
Drive Alert
Easy Lift Model 1
Fireban
Knight Hawk II Car Alarm

Radar Detector Mirror
Sav-A-Life
Spotlight Inflator

LILLIAN VERNON:
Light-up Reader

SECURITY

BROOKSTONE:
Book-Safe
Key Stone

DAK INDUSTRIES:
Electronic Flyswatter

EXETERS:
Phone Guard
Sound Activated Light Switch

HAMMACHER SCHLEMMER:
Portable Door Alarm
Portable Electric Baby Sitter
The Thinking Wallet
Travel Jewelry Protector

HEATHKIT:
Heat Sniffer
Intelligent Thermostats

INNOVATIONS:
Beep-N-Keep Key Finder
Blaze-Out Fire Extinguisher
Challenger Rechargeable Floodlight
Driveway Alert
Light Alert
Nutone Wireless Door Chime
Sentry Security Chest
Talking Watch

THE KIDS

HAMMACHER SCHLEMMER:
Prenatal Sound Lamb

INNOVATIONS:
Amphibian 110 Underwater Camera

LILLIAN VERNON:
Computerized Piggy Bank

TOYS TO GROW ON:
Deluxe Safety Sitter
Safety Bath Whale
Socket Lock-it

THE OFFICE

CASIO:
Casio Card Radio
Casio Credit Card Calculator

EXETERS:
Command Dialer Phone

HAMMACHER SCHLEMMER:
Automatic Paper Shredder
The Only Folding Printing Calculator
Stock Market Monitor

INNOVATIONS:
Easytalk Headset Headband
Electronic Dictionary Typewriter
World Clock

FOR THE MILLIONAIRE

CCS COMMUNICATIONS CONTROL INC.:
Secret Connection Briefcase

HAMMACHER SCHLEMMER:
The Ascot Umbrella Seat-Stick
Chesalturf Putting Green
English Putter Flask
Osaka Electric Massage/Stereo Chair
Schmeckenbecker Putter
17-in-One Golf Club
Solar-Powered Ventilated Pith Helmet
Traveling Stereo Attache
The World's Only Computerized Fishing Reel

INNOVATIONS:
Golf N'Go II
Stroke Saver

TRAVEL

BROOKSTONE:
Travel Clock & Smoke Alarm
Traveler's Water Heater

HAMMACHER SCHLEMMER:
Cordless, Compact Travel Lamp
Self-Cleaning Travel Iron

INNOVATIONS:
International Travelers Converter Kit

Index